FANTASTIC
500
PUZZLE
CHALLENGE

THIS IS A CARLTON BOOK

Design copyright © Carlton Publishing Group 2006
Unless otherwise stated all puzzles © 2004, 2006 Puzzler Media Limited, RH1 1EY
www.puzzler.co.uk

The following puzzles are the copyright of Nikoli (http://www.nikoli.co.jp):
6, 12, 14, 19, 23, 39, 49, 51, 70, 76, 77, 88, 92, 101, 110, 120, 136, 141, 143,
158, 166, 176, 182, 185, 188, 202, 209, 212, 221, 222, 223, 236, 237, 238, 245,
250, 252, 253, 260, 263, 265, 274, 281, 289, 301, 312, 313, 332, 339, 342, 344,
347, 356, 361, 387, 390, 403, 408, 413, 420, 445, 483, 497

This edition published in 2006 by Carlton Books Ltd
A Division of the Carlton Publishing Group
20 Mortimer Street
London W1T 3JW

A CIP catalogue record for this book is available from the British Library

ISBN 13: 978-0-68145-368-5
ISBN 10: 0-68145-368-0

Printed in Dubai

FANTASTIC
500
PUZZLE
CHALLENGE

General Editor: Robert Allen

SEVENOAKS

INTRODUCTION

It seems that people just can't get enough of puzzles so, whether you fancy tackling a quick teaser or puzzling over something more challenging, this book is bound to include just what you need. More than 500 puzzles are featured and they make up a really impressive and varied collection that will provide you with hours of endless mind-boggling moments. Puzzles range from picture puzzles – such as spot the differences and the odd one out – logic problems, and visual reasoning enigmas to number problems, including the ever popular Sudoku, mazes, physical problems and mathematical crosswords. You can browse through the book for five minutes and solve a quick puzzle or spend a whole day on one of the real biggies. It's entirely up to you. Each puzzle has been awarded a level of difficulty, indicated by dots next to their headings, so the more dots there are, the more difficult and time-consuming the puzzle will be. But don't be put off by a hard puzzle! The difficulty is purely subjective and you may find that you breeze through those with the more difficult rating. However, in cases where the solutions are proving to be elusive, the answers can always be found at the back of the book. Happy puzzling!

THE PUZZLES

1 TENTACKLE

Eight children are camping, two to each tent, and some have given us a couple of clues as to how to find them. The trouble is their directions are as bad as their cooking and in each case only one direction is true whilst the other is an exact opposite, so that East should read West etc. Directions are not necessarily exact so North could be North, Northeast or Northwest. To help you one child is already tucked into a sleeping bag.

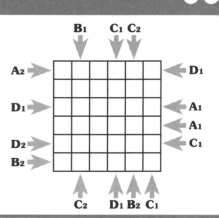

Alvin says: "I'm East of Harvey and South of Dexter."
Dexter says: "I'm West of Frank and North of Elmer."
Frank says: "I'm West of Conrad and North of Brad."
Gary says: "I'm West of Elmer and South of Harvey."

2 CODE MASTER

Just follow the rules of that classic puzzle, Master Mind, to crack the number code. The first number tells you how many of the digits are exactly correct – the right digit in the right place (✓✓). The second number tells you how many digits are the correct number but are not in the right place (✓). By comparing the information given by each line, can you work out which number goes in which place?

					✓✓	✓
3	1	0	4	5	1	1
0	8	1	9	2	0	2
1	4	5	9	7	1	3
3	6	4	5	7	1	2
4	5	2	8	6	1	1

3 EASY AS ABC

Each row and column originally contained one A, one B, one C, one D and two blank squares. Each letter and number refers to the first or second of the four letters encountered when travelling in the direction of the arrow. Can you complete the original grid?

4 CARDS ON THE TABLE

The 13 cards of a suit plus 2 Jokers are shuffled and dealt in a line. No two consecutive cards are adjacent, no Joker or court card is at either end, and no two court cards are adjacent.

Ace is two places left of Queen, 2 is two places left of 8, one Joker two left of 3, the other Joker somewhere left of both, and between 6 (left) and 10. 7 is two left of 4, Jack two right of King, 5 somewhere right of 9, which is somewhere right of 7, which is somewhere right of 10.

Ace is left of 7.

The 7th and 10th cards from the left are even (Ace = 1, King = 13, Q = 12, Jack = 11 and a Joker is neither odd nor even). The Queen is left of the King. The 3rd and 10th cards from the left total 12, as do the 8th and 15th.

Can you locate each card?

5 NETWORK

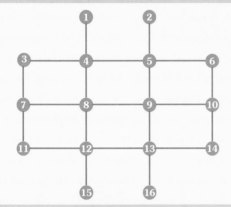

The letters A–P are to be arranged in the diagram, with one letter allocated to each point, so that no two consecutive letters are connected by any direct line i.e., 1–15 or 7–10. F is to the left of, and in the same horizontal line as I, which is above C. H and D are both somewhere left of B though not necessarily in the same line. P is somewhere higher than J, O somewhere higher than F, H somewhere higher than M and L somewhere higher than E but not necessarily in the same line.

B is diagonally adjacent to G and A is diagonally adjacent to C. N is the greatest distance possible from O.

L is immediately left of I, G immediately left of K, J immediately left of C and D immediately left of O.

If the positions of the letters E and F add up to 17 can you place each letter in its correct position?

6 DOTTY DILEMMA

Connect adjacent dots with vertical or horizontal lines so that a single loop is formed with no crossings or branches. Each number indicates how many lines surround it, while empty cells may be surrounded by any number of lines.

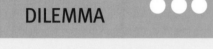

```
· · 3.2.3 · · 1.2.3 · · 1.2.
2· · · · · · · 0· · · · 1.1· ·
0· · · · · · 2· · · · · · · 3·
· 1· · 3.0· · · · 2· · · 3· ·
· 1· · · 1.0· · 0· · · 2· · ·
· 3· · 0.1· · · 3· · · · · · ·
· 1· · · · 1· · · 1· · 1.1.3·
· · 0· · · · · 2· · · 3· · · ·
0· · 3· · 3.3· · · 2· · · 2· ·
1· · 2· · · · 2.2· · · 2· 0· ·
2· · · 3· · · · · 3· · 1· · 3·
· · · 3· · 3.2· · 2· · · · · ·
· · · · 2· · 1.3· · · 1· · · ·
· · 3· · 1· · 3· · · · · · · 1·
1· · 2· · · · · · · · · · · 3·
· 1· · · · 1· · 1.3· · · 3.1· ·
· 1· · · 2· · · 1.0· · 1· · 0·
· · · 2· · · · 1· · · 2· · · ·
1.3.2· · 2· · · · 2· · · 1· · ·
· · · 1· · · · 3.2· · · 2· · ·
· · 3· · 0· · 1· · · · · · 1· ·
· 3· · 3· · · · · · 0.2· · 2· ·
· · · · · 2· · · 2· · · · · 2·
· · 1.1· · · 1· · · 1· · · · 0·
·1.0· · · 1.3.2· · · 0.2.3·
```

8 POLICE SQUAD

Siren screaming, Frank Drabin pulled his squad car into the side of the road, demolishing three trash cans and a pizza stand. He raced into the building, gun drawn, took the stairs three at a time and gave them back two at a time. Finally he turned into a square hallway and crouched down behind an aspidistra.
"What have we got, Ed?"
A nearby rubber plant shook its leaves.
"We got a gunman or gunmen, Frank. We also have one informer who tipped us off."
"Where are they?"
"We're not sure – but somewhere in the five rooms leading off this landing."
"Well, just open 'em up one at a time and go in blasting."
"No can do, Frank. We've almost used our quota of bullets for the month and we don't want to hit the informer."
"I see someone's been playing games – put notices on the doors."
"Yeah – before we got here. They're trying to confuse us."
"Each stuck a note on his door and maybe on an empty door as well.
The notice on the informer's door is entirely true. The notice on any gunman's door is completely false."
"And the empty rooms?"
"The notice may be either entirely true or entirely false."
"So where's the gunman/men?"

Rm 2 has a gunman. Rm 4 is empty. **1**

Room 1 is empty. The note on door 4 is false. **2**

There is a gunman in Rm 5. Rm 2 is empty. **3**

Rm 3 is empty. The informer is in Rm 2. **4**

The sign on door 3 is false. The informer is in Rm 2. **5**

7 TALENT SPOTTING

Once the electronic scoreboard had fused at Mutlins Camp Talent Night, chaos was the result. Later that evening, six Purple Coats stopped smiling at holidaymakers and tried to work out the score. Here's what each thought:

The dancer was 6th. The escapologist won.
The impressionist was 4th. The magician was 6th.
The escapologist was 3rd. The baritone was 6th.

The baritone was 4th. The comedian was 3rd.
The dancer was 4th. The magician was 2nd.
The dancer was 5th. The comedian was 4th.

Each actually had one position correct and one wrong in his/her pair of statements. At that point, they gave up. But with your puzzling skill, can you work out the place in which each contestant finished?

9 PARTY TIME ● ●

Party time and the table is all set up with eight coloured cakes in position waiting for the children to sit down and tuck in. From the information below can you work out where each child will be sitting?

At Lisa's birthday party boys and girls are alternately seated. Tom has the yellow cake on one side and is opposite a 'D' child. John and Jenny are next to each other but neither is next to the blue cake. Moira has the orange cake on one side and Dan on the other. Moira is not opposite Gwen who is not next to Dick.

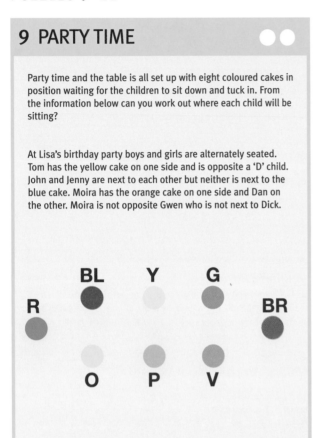

11 LOGI-5 ● ●

Each line, across and down, is to have each of the five colours appearing once each. Each colour must also appear just once in each shape, shown by thick lines. Can you colour in this crazy quilt, or mark each square with its correct letter B, G, R, V or Y?

10 NUMBER KROSS

See how quickly you can fit all these numbers into the grid. We've filled one number in to start you off.

3 figures		
115	17926	393794
242	21223	403958
301	22107	455514
429	32379	503040
706	37135	514171
743	41327	644721
816	41670	671517
929	51078	701419
	53071	715926
	60606	804717
4 figures	71230	958473
1557	72325	981739
2154	80128	
3918	91837	
4177	91917	
5172		
6855		
7050	6 figures	
9230	107000	
	167245	
5 figures	214412	
10201	314253	

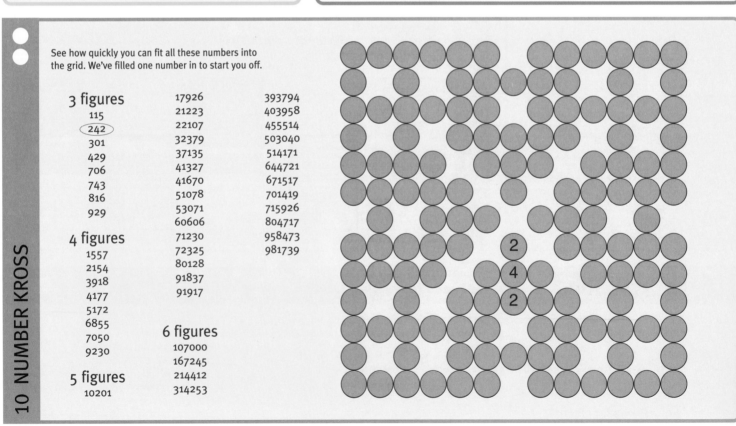

Travel from the entrance to the exit of the maze, filling the path completely to create a picture.

12 MAZE MYSTERY

13 ALL OF A FLUTTER

Bean's fancy-dress costume has attracted lots of butterflies! Can you see which type of butterfly is the only one to appear three times in this picture?

14 CELL STRUCTURE

Each circle containing a number represents an island. The object is to connect each island with vertical or horizontal bridges so that:

* The number of bridges is the same as the number inside the island.
* There can be up to two . bridges between two islands
* Bridges cannot cross islands or other bridges.
* There is a continuous path connecting all the islands.

15 EASY AS ABC

Each row and column originally contained one A, one B, one C, one D and two blank squares. Each letter and number refers to the first or second of the four letters encountered when travelling in the direction of the arrow. Can you complete the original grid?

16 FRUIT AND VEG

The display on Gert's stall is changed around daily, partly to make yesterday's produce look fresh. Whatever the arrangement, fruit and vegetables always alternate along the rows and down the lines and left and right are as you gaze on wondering if you have the nerve to ask if the dates are ripe. The turnips are one line to the right of the bananas which are in the same line down as the marrows which are in the same line across as the lychees which are not in the same line across as the potatoes which are directly above the apples which are further to the left and lower than the peas which are directly below the cherries which are two lines to the right of the yams which are higher than and one place to the left of the watercress which is directly to the left of the kumquats which are one line down from the grapes which are two lines to the right of the figs which are higher than but not in the same line down as the radishes which are one place below and one place to the right of the turnips which are three rows higher than the illustrated onions.

17 NUMBER KROSS

3 figures	5 figures	6 figures
152	10576	101316
234	20231	210211
387	23327	252426
489	30213	305306
516	37733	395446
(650)	40006	414342
713	41425	420395
834	50139	515253
	50289	537219
4 figures	61577	625773
1918	63414	636669
2227	70318	747176
3514	71902	773355
4530	78470	817512
5995	80817	918317
6130	91532	995033
7476		
8104		

See how quickly you can fit all these numbers into the grid. We've filled one number in to start you off.

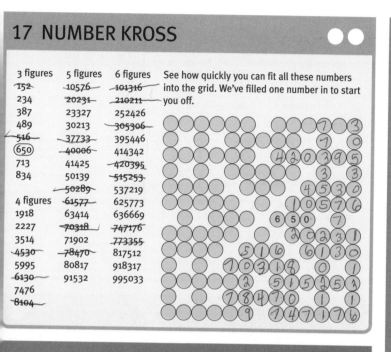

18 LINE UP

Can you follow a continuous black line in this picture from the arrow by the camera to the arrow by the bird's tail? No jumping over gaps!

19 DOTTING DILEMMA

Connect adjacent dots with vertical or horizontal lines so that a single loop is formed with no crossings or branches. Each number indicates how many lines surround it, while empty cells may be surrounded by any number of lines.

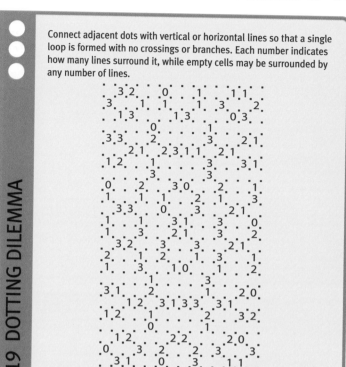

20 ARMS AND THE MAN

The Grand-Duke Hans Niess-und-Bumpzer-Dazi had a very long pedigree, giving rise to the four quarterings on his coat-of-arms. From the clues given below, can you name the creature depicted in each of the quarters numbered 1 to 4, say in which colour it is displayed, and name the Middle-European family whose arms were introduced into the Grand-Duke's family's as a result of various dynastic marriages over the centuries?

Clues

1 The pink elephant, badge of a family of noted drinkers, appears in the quarter directly above the one inherited from the Klotzky family arms.

2 The creature which is depicted in black has appeared on the Grand-Ducal arms since Hans' grandfather married the eldest daughter of Count von Plonka.

3 The lion of the Muddelkopfs, which is not orange, is to be seen in an odd-numbered quarter of the arms.

4 The dragon is immediately to the right of the blue creature.

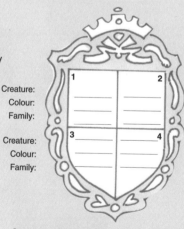

Creature:
Colour:
Family:

Creature:
Colour:
Family:

Creatures: dragon; eagle; elephant; lion
Colours: black; blue; orange; pink
Families: Klotzky; Muddelkopf; Nitwitz; von Plonka

Starting tip: Begin by identifying the creature depicted in quarter number 4.

21 TEE TIME

Three old timers play a weekly game of golf on the Golden Lawns 18-hole, par 72, course. Each score at every hole falls into one of five categories. Each golfer gets a different result, greater than zero in each category. Also, no category has the same result for another player, i.e., if a players has two eagles, he has a different number in the other four and no other player has two eagles. With the score details below and the information given, can you fill in their card?

	Eagle −2	Birdie −1	Par 0	Bogey +1	Double Bogey +2	FINAL SCORE
Parnell Darma						
Nick Jackliss						
Barry Clayer						

Barry scored one more par than bogeys and together they came to one more than Nick's pars. Nick got both the most eagles and double bogeys and together they equalled Parnell's pars. Barry got twice as many birdies as Nick did eagles and these were two less than Parnell's birdies. Altogether there were 20 pars. The total number of birdies was two less than the total number of bogeys and double bogeys. Nick's birdie score was not the same as either Parnell's bogey score or Barry's double bogey score.

22 SHORT AND SNAPPY

Can you tell which of the five shadows is that belonging to the puppy in the top left-hand corner?

A

B

C

D

E

23 CELL STRUCTURE

Place a number from 1 to 9 in each empty cell so that the sum of each vertical or horizontal block equals the number at the top or on the left of that block. Numbers may only be used once in each block.

24 BATTLESHIPS

Do you remember the old game of battleships? These puzzles are based on that idea. Your task is to find the vessels in the diagram. Some parts of boats or sea squares have already been filled in, and a number next to a row or column refers to the number of occupied squares in that row or column. The boats may be positioned horizontally or vertically, but no two boats or parts of boats are in adjacent squares – horizontally, vertically or diagonally.

Aircraft carrier:

Battleships:

Cruisers:

Destroyers:

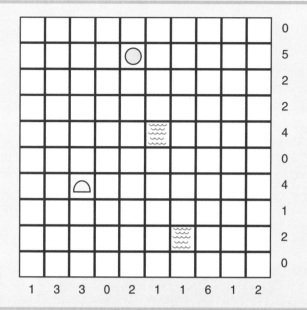

25 FLOWER POWER

There are eight differences between these two pictures – can you spot them?

26 ON COURSE

Four employees at Hall-Thumms Digital Co, have recently taken work-related courses run by Gerta Leggup's Updating Agency. From the clues, can you give, with a high degree of confidence, a summary showing each employee's name, course and cost?

Clues
1. Zebedee's course cost $200 less than Dougal's which cost $50 less than Holmes' which cost $200 more than was paid for Speedy Searching.
2. Brian's course cost more than Wexford's which, at $400 per day, was not the cheapest.
3. Advanced Surfing cost $200 more than Brown's course which cost $50 less than Florence's.
4. Dalgliesh's course cost $50 less than Novice Newsgroup which cost $250 more than Browsing For Beginners.

FORENAME	SURNAME	COURSE	COST
Brian			
Dougal			
Florence			
Zebedee			

27 CARDS ON THE TABLE

The 13 cards of a suit, plus two jokers, are shuffled and dealt in a line. No suit card is in its correct position, counting left to right, whether you begin with the Ace or both the Jokers. No court cards are adjacent to each other or to any Joker.

There is one card separating the Jokers, which are both right of all the court cards and Ace, one of which is on the extreme left. 8 is two places left of 9, Ace two left of 3, 6 two left of 2, Queen two left of Jack, 10 two left of 8, 4 three left of the first Joker from the left, King three left of Ace, 6 four left of 5, first Joker four right of the Queen.

The 4th, 7th and 10th cards from the left are odd, the 5th, 9th and 13th are even (Jokers are neither odd nor even).

Can you locate each card?

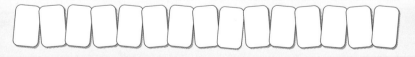

28 BREAKTHROUGH

See how quickly you can break this grid down into the 28 dominoes from which it is formed.

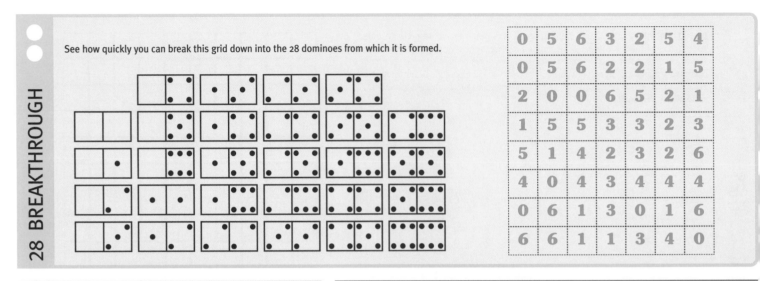

0	5	6	3	2	5	4
0	5	6	2	2	1	5
2	0	0	6	5	2	1
1	5	5	3	3	2	3
5	1	4	2	3	2	6
4	0	4	3	4	4	4
0	6	1	3	0	1	6
6	6	1	1	3	4	0

29 EASY AS ABC

Each row and column in this grid originally contained one A, one B, one C, one D and two blank squares. Each black letter refers to the first of the four letters encountered when travelling in the direction of the arrow, while each blue circled letter refers to the second of the four letters encountered when travelling in the direction of the arrow. Can you complete the original grid?

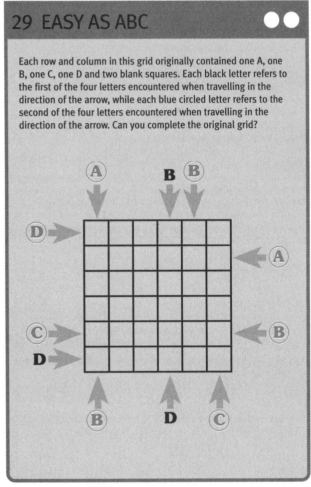

30 SHADY CHARACTER

Shade in every part of this picture that contains a vowel. What do you see?

31 AGEING FAST

Sam's mother is 63. How old is Sam if her mother is now three times as old as Sam was when her mother was as old as Sam is now? Quick – before they get any older!

32 IN THE ABSTRACT

The Museum of Modern Sculpture in Storbury has a small gallery devoted to the work of abstract sculptor Ivor Screwloose. From the clues given below, can you name the works lettered A to D in the diagram, and say in which season of which year each was produced?

Clues

1 Sculpture B represents *Dichotomy*, perhaps reflecting Ivor's state of mind in the non-leap year in which it was sculpted.

2 *Enchantment* was completed in Fall.

3 *Sorrow* was not sculpted in 1994.

4 As you look at the diagram, the sculpture named *Revenge* was completed two years after the one to its left, but earlier than the Spring sculpture, which is somewhere to its right.

5 None of the works was completed in the Summer of 1992.

Sculptures: *Dichotomy; Enchantment; Revenge; Sorrow*
Seasons: Spring; Summer; Fall; Winter
Years: 1990; 1992; 1994; 1996

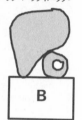
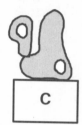
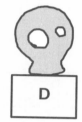

A   B   C   D

Name: _____ _____ _____ _____

Season: _____ _____ _____ _____

Year: _____ _____ _____ _____

Starting tip: Begin by placing *Revenge*.

33 FLYING HIGH

Can you see which of these five balloons contains two of each of the different symbols?

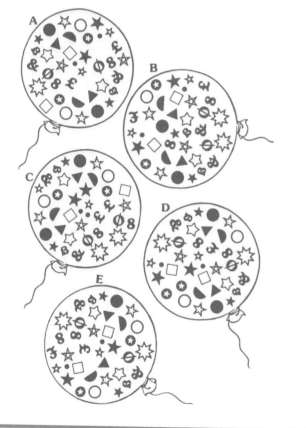

34 CODE MASTER

Just follow the rules of that classic puzzle Master Mind, to crack the number code. The first number tells you how many of the digits are exactly correct – the right digit in the right place (✓✓). The second number tells you how many digits are the correct number but are not in the right place (✓). By comparing the information given by each line, can you work out which number goes in which place?

					✓✓	✓
6	5	2	7	1	1	2
4	3	0	8	9	1	0
9	1	2	5	9	1	3
3	0	1	7	4	2	0
6	3	7	6	2	0	2

35 FILLING IN

Each of the nine empty boxes contains a *different* digit from 1 to 9. Each calculation is to be treated sequentially rather than according to the 'multiplication first' system. Can you fill in the empty boxes?

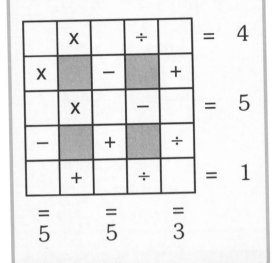

36 CROSSNUMBER QUICKIE

1A = 122 x 5A
5A is a prime number
6A = 101 x 4A
1D = 101 x 5D
2D is a square number
3D = 4A x 2D
7, 8 and 9 do not appear in the solution.

Historical clue: Death of Shakespeare.
The year can be read in the lightly shaded squares.

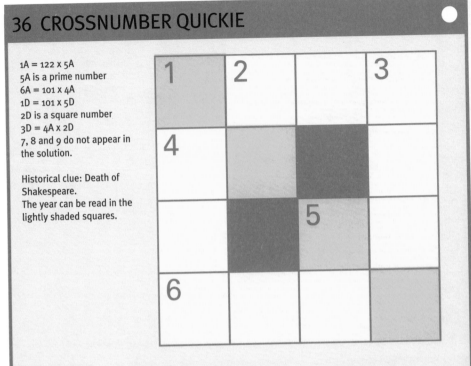

37 ROSES, ROSES

The delivery boy at Just Blooms flower shop was told to take half a dozen dozen roses to the wedding of Ms Green and six dozen dozen to the silver wedding of Mrs Grey. Knowing that six is half a dozen he delivered the same number to each place. Did he do right?

38 IN THE CLOUDS

Which one of the numbered lines leads to this cloud?

Travel from the entrance to the exit of the maze, filling the path completely to create a picture.

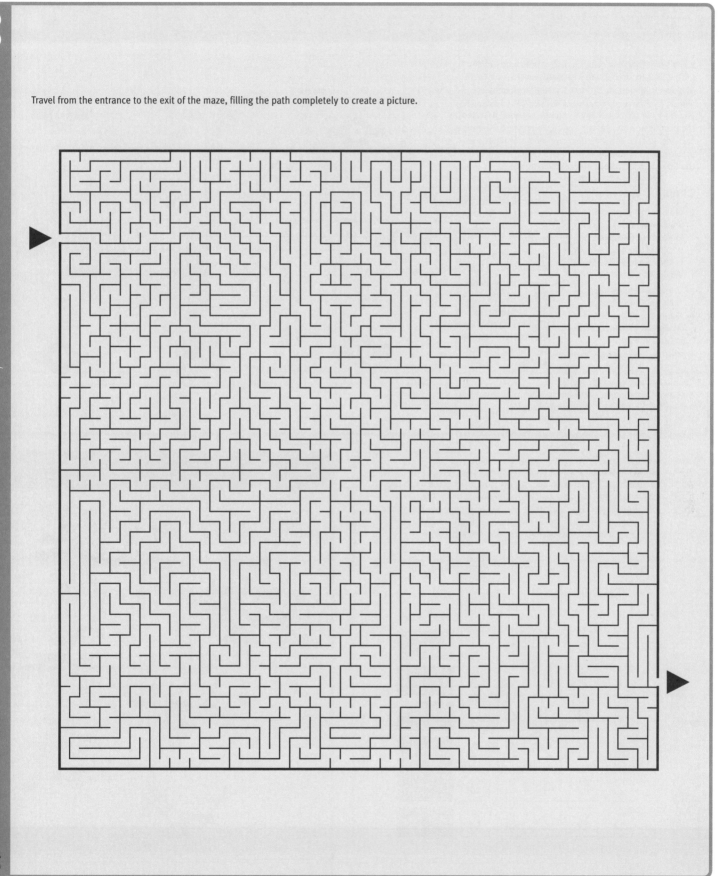

40 ACTION STATIONS

A city's Metro system consists of four lines, one running north to south, one east to west, and two crossing these diagonally, all passing through the central interchange station at Nelson Square. From the clues given below, can you work out the colour in which lines 1 to 4 are depicted on the plan posted up at every station, and name the terminus stations on each line, entering your answers in the spaces provided? NB The terms western and eastern apply to any of the three termini in each of those directions.

Clues

1 One of the diagonal lines runs from The Unicorn to Gradwell, which is the next terminus clockwise from Wallgate.

2 The blue line forms a right angle at Nelson Square with the one whose western terminus is Molton Park.

3 The red line bears a number two higher than the one whose eastern terminus is Riverhead.

4 Potterfield is indicated on the plan by a letter two further down the alphabet than Lampwick.

5 Castlebridge is not on the green line.

6 The two terminus stations on the blue line do not have names containing the same number of letters.

Colours: blue; green; red; yellow
Stations: Castlebridge; Gradwell; Lampwick; Molton Park; Potterfield; Riverhead; The Unicorn; Wallgate

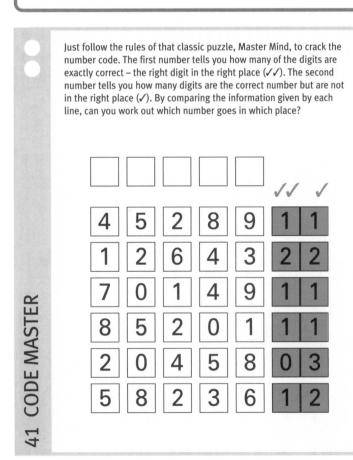

Name: _____
Name: _____
Name: _____
Line 1 – Colour: _____
Line 4 – Colour: _____
Nelson Square
Line 3 – Colour: _____
Line 2 – Colour: _____
Name: _____
Name: _____
Name: _____
Name: _____
Name: _____

Starting tip: Begin by working out which station is Riverhead.

41 CODE MASTER

Just follow the rules of that classic puzzle, Master Mind, to crack the number code. The first number tells you how many of the digits are exactly correct – the right digit in the right place (✓✓). The second number tells you how many digits are the correct number but are not in the right place (✓). By comparing the information given by each line, can you work out which number goes in which place?

					✓✓	✓
4	5	2	8	9	1	1
1	2	6	4	3	2	2
7	0	1	4	9	1	1
8	5	2	0	1	1	1
2	0	4	5	8	0	3
5	8	2	3	6	1	2

42 ODD ONE OUT

Which one of these panicky cats is different from all the others?

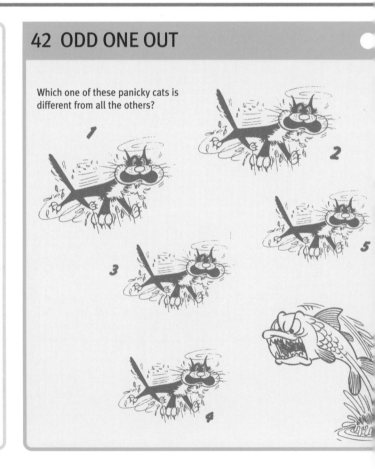

43 FAIR PRICE

Simple Simon met a pieman, going to the fair. Said Simple Simon to the pieman, "How much is your ware?" Said the pieman to Simple Simon, "It's seven pennies for each of these, and eight pennies for each of those." Simple Simon paid ninety seven pennies, for some of these and some of those. How many of each had he chosen?

44 SEVEN ALL

7 x 7 is 49

So, without using a calculator, just how quickly can you find the answer to:

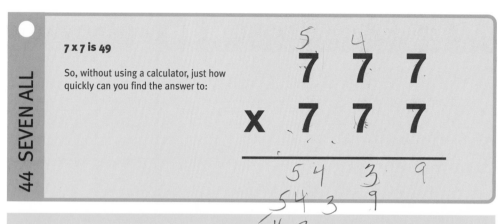

$$\begin{array}{r} 777 \\ \times\ 777 \\ \hline \end{array}$$

(handwritten working):
```
      5   4
  7   7   7
x 7   7   7
─────────────
  5 4   3   9
  5 4 3   9
  5 4 3 9
6 0 3 7 2 9
```

45 FILLING IN

Each of the nine empty boxes contains a digit from 1 to 9. As is our usual practice, each calculation is to be treated sequentially rather than according to the 'multiplication and division first' system. Can you fill in the empty boxes?

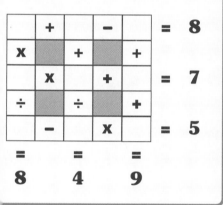

	+		−		=	8
x		+		+		
	x		+		=	7
÷		÷		+		
	−		x		=	5
=		=		=		
8		4		9		

46 WHAT A KNIGHTMARE

Join the dots from 1 to 135 to find out why this nervous knight wishes he'd stayed at home this morning.

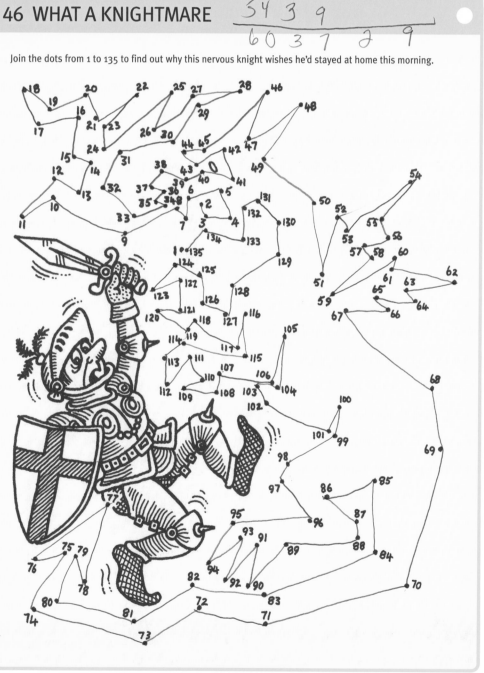

47 BATTLESHIPS ● ● ●

Do you remember the old game of battleships? This puzzle is based on that idea. Your task is to find the six vessels in the diagram. Some parts of boats or sea squares have already been filled in, and a number next to a row or column refers to the number of occupied squares in that row or column. A row or column with nothing next to it does not necessarily mean that there are no ship parts there. The boats may be positioned horizontally or vertically, but no two boats or parts of boats are in adjacent squares – horizontally, vertically or diagonally.

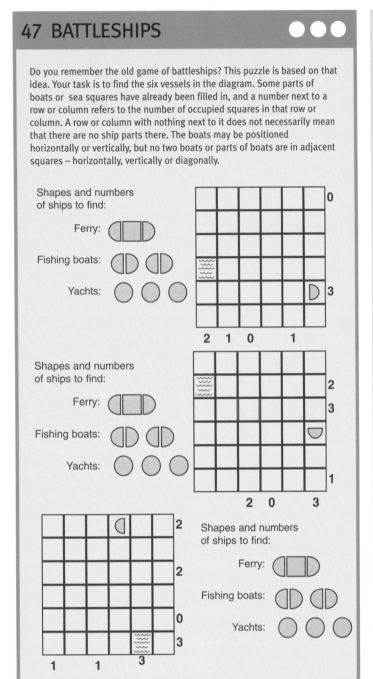

Shapes and numbers of ships to find:

Ferry:

Fishing boats:

Yachts:

Shapes and numbers of ships to find:

Ferry:

Fishing boats:

Yachts:

Shapes and numbers of ships to find:

Ferry:

Fishing boats:

Yachts:

48 CASTING LOTS ● ● ●

Peregrine Cupick, who had had some experience as a professional provincial theatre director, came on retirement to live in Netherlipp and offered his services to the Netherlipp Players, who, duly impressed, acceded to his casting decisions for his first production of A Midsummer Night's Dream with unprecedented docility. However, the roles he assigned to the five leading male members were not the ones they had hoped for and he had tried them out at a reading round a table; from the clues given below, can you work out which actor sat where, what part he was given and which role he would have preferred?

Clues

1 Lime sat next clockwise after the man who had aspired to be Quince and opposite the one who was given the part of Demetrius.

2 Pitt's place was next clockwise after that of the man chosen to be Lysander and opposite that of the one who wanted to be Lysander.

3 The man cast as Oberon was next left to the one who got the part of Demetrius; the latter was opposite the actor who had set his heart on being Oberon.

4 Lynes sat next right to the man who wanted to play Bottom and opposite the one who was given the role of Quince.

5 Green was next clockwise after the selected Bottom and next anti-clockwise from the selected Oberon and was opposite the actor who was next left to the would-be Quince.

Actors: Flood; Green; Lime; Lynes; Pitt
Roles: Bottom; Demetrius; Lysander; Oberon; Quince

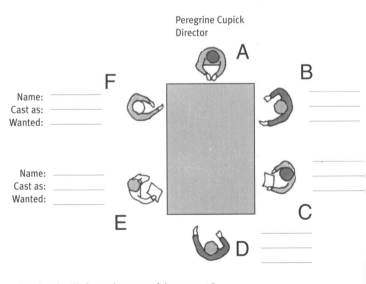

Peregrine Cupick
Director

Name:
Cast as:
Wanted:

Name:
Cast as:
Wanted:

Starting tip: Work out the name of the actor at D.

49 SUDOKU ● ● ●

Place a number from 1 to 9 in each empty cell so that each row, each column and each 3 x 3 block contains all the numbers from 1 to 9.

3				5				
	9	6	8					
	1			4				7
	6		2					
	7	5				1	3	
				9			4	
2				3			8	
				1	7	9		
		4						6

50 STAMP COLLECTION

Which one of the numbered marks has been made with this stamp?

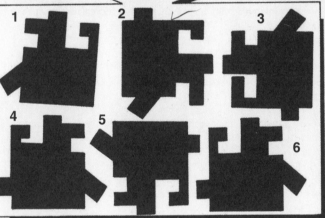

51 DOTTY DILEMMA

Connect adjacent dots with vertical or horizontal lines so that a single loop is formed with no crossings or branches. Each number indicates how many lines surround it, while empty cells may be surrounded by any number of lines.

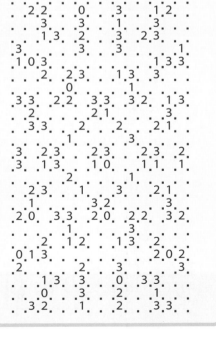

52 BATTLESHIPS

Do you remember the old game of battleships? These puzzles are based on that idea. Your task is to find the vessels in the diagram. Some parts of boats or sea squares have already been filled in, and a number next to a row or column refers to the number of occupied squares in that row or column. A row or column with nothing next to it does not necessarily mean that there are no ship parts there. The boats may be positioned horizontally or vertically, but no two boats or parts of boats are in adjacent squares – horizontally, vertically or diagonally.

Shapes and numbers of ships to find:

Oil tanker:
Ferries:
Fishing boats:
Yachts:

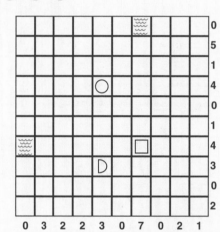

Now try these two smaller, but no less tricky, versions of Battleships.

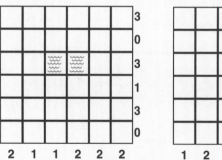
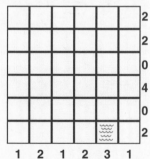

Shapes and numbers of ships to find:

Ferry:

Fishing boats:

Yachts:

53 ALL ABOARD

Which one of the numbered prints was made from the stamp?

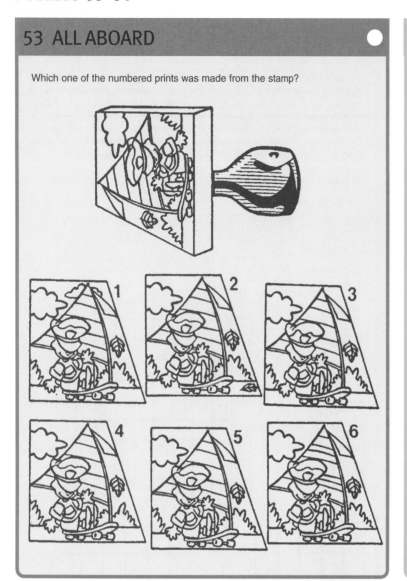

54 THE NUMBERS GAME

Each of the squares in the diagram numbered 1 to 6 contains one of those six numbers, one of the first six letters of the alphabet, and one of the Roman numbers I to VI. From the clues given below, can you place the correct three items in each square?

Clues

1 Taking the six letters A to F as representing their numerical position in the alphabet, none of the squares contains its own letter or number of either type, and no two equivalent numbers or letters appear in any of the squares.

2 The C is in the square immediately to the left of the Roman II.

3 The D appears in the square above that containing the 4. The B is in the square above that containing the III.

4 The 3 is in the square above the VI. The 5 is not in square 2.

5 The 6 appears in the same square as the V. The F appears in the same square as the IV. The I appears in the same square as the E.

6 The Arabic number in square 5 is larger than its Roman companion.

Numbers: 1; 2; 3; 4; 5; 6
Letters: A; B; C; D; E; F
Roman numbers: I; II; III IV; V; VI

	1	2	3
Arabic:	___	___	___
Letter:	___	___	___
Roman:	___	___	___
	4	5	6
Arabic:	___	___	___
Letter:	___	___	___
Roman:	___	___	___

Starting tip: Start by placing the Roman VI.

55 CODE MASTER

Just follow the rules of that classic puzzle, Master Mind, to crack the number code. The first number tells you how many of the digits are exactly correct – the right digit in the right place (✓✓). The second number tells you how many digits are the correct number but are not in the right place (✓). By comparing the information given by each line, can you work out which number goes in which place?

					✓✓	✓
9	5	8	3	4	0	1
7	8	6	0	2	2	2
2	7	8	5	3	1	2
4	6	3	8	2	1	2
6	3	2	7	5	0	3
1	9	4	0	6	0	2

56 IT'S MAGIC

This magic square can be completed using the numbers from 32 to 56 inclusive. To give you a start the first row has all its even digits entered, the second row all its odd digits, the third row even again, the fourth odd and the fifth even. Can you complete the square so that the five numbers in each row, column, and diagonal add up to the magic total? The total—close your eyes if you don't want to be told—is 220.

	2		4 6	4 8	
5 1	5 3	3 5	3 7	
4 0	4 2	4		6
5	3	3	5	7
4	0	2	4 4	

57 SNAKES AND LADDERS

Which one of the lettered cubes can be made from the unfolded pattern?

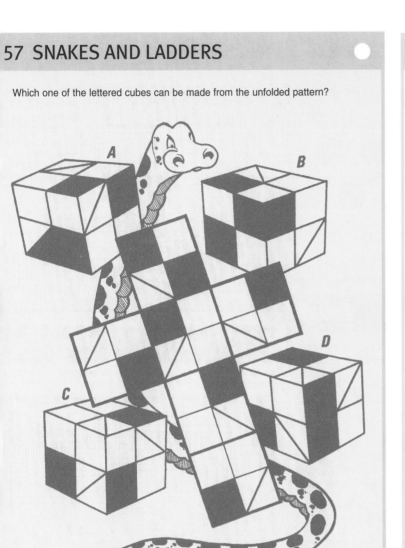

59 NUMBER KROSS

See how quickly you can fit all these numbers into the grid. We've filled one number in to start you off.

3 figures
142
216
425
511
635
732
848
920

4 figures
1968
2075
3545

4656
5483
6122
7901
8234

5 figures
16539
17822
27383
29743
34551
37894
42345

43049
57182
66278
66978
73842
74256
83445
88640
96780

6 figures
120816
134565

206317
241327
367687
423458
454288
519619
637452
678902
767893
775406
822538
862728
904111
941157

58 CHANGING PLACES

Do you recall Alice's cleaning lady who never puts things back in their proper places? This week it was the six cushions on Alice's capacious sofa which she relocated. From the clues given below, can you establish their original and revised positions?

Clues

1 The gold cushion was moved as many places to the right as the red was to the left; the green was moved in the same direction as the gold, but by a shorter distance, while the pink was moved one fewer place to the left than the red.

2 The green took the place of the turquoise and the turquoise the place of the blue, moving one fewer place left than the blue did right, but more than one more than the green.

3 Neither the green nor the turquoise was at either end both before and after the cleaning operation; the green should have been next left to the turquoise but finished up more than two places to the right of it; the blue should have been next left to the pink but finished up more than two places to the right of it.

4 Alice would never have placed the pink and red next to each other.

Colours: blue, gold, green, pink, red, turquoise

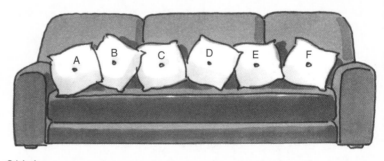

Original: _____ _____ _____ _____ _____ _____

New: _____ _____ _____ _____ _____ _____

Starting tip: Work out the original colour of the cushion at F.

25

60 SQUARED AWAY

In how many different ways can these three pieces form a 3 x 3 square? The pieces are numbered on the front and the back, so they can be turned over. Rotations and reflections of the final numbered square are not counted as different.

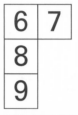

61 NEXT NUMBER

What number belongs in the circle marked ?

7 21 35 49

41 82 24 ?

62 SEARCH PARTY

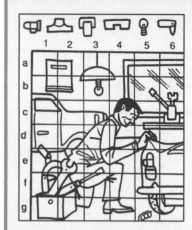

Four of the six shapes at the top can be found in the main picture. Can you spot their whereabouts?

64 IT CAME TO PASS

The diagram illustrates a delightful passing movement involving seven members of a soccer team during a recent televised match. From the clues given below, can you work out the names of the seven players who took part in the move in their correct order?

Clues

1 Garry, who was in the opponents' half of the field, received a pass from O'Casey.

2 Clyde Johnson received the ball from Darren, and passed it to Marchant.

3 Steve is the player numbered 2 in the diagram.

4 David, who is not the goalkeeper, was the provider of the telling pass to Mike, who is not in the same half of the pitch as Bennett.

5 Peter, who received the ball from Glenn, was not the provider of the pass received by Donovan.

6 Swann is the surname of the player numbered 3 in the diagram.

First names: Clyde; Darren; David; Garry; Mike; Peter; Steve
Surnames: Bennett; Donovan; Glenn; Johnson; Marchant; O'Casey; Swann

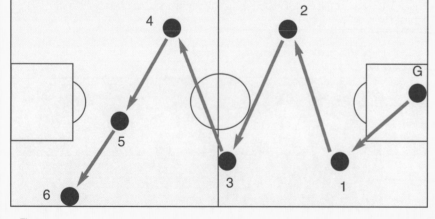

First name: _____ _____ _____ _____ _____ _____ _____

Surname: _____ _____ _____ _____ _____ _____ _____

Starting tip: Begin by working out the first name of the goalkeeper who started the move.

63 WIRED UP

Which of the four plugs should be inserted in the socket to operate the razor?

65 DOT-TO-DOT

Join the dots from 1 to 33 to reveal the hidden picture.

66 BLACK OUT

Can you decide which three of the fifteen vases are shown in silhouette at the top?

68 CODE MASTER

Just follow the rules of that classic puzzle, Master Mind, to crack the number code. The first number tells you how many of the digits are exactly correct – the right digit in the right place (✓✓). The second number tells you how many digits are the correct number but are not in the right place (✓). By comparing the information given by each line, can you work out which number goes in which place?

					✓✓	✓
5	4	2	7	0	2	0
8	4	2	3	1	0	2
1	9	5	2	8	0	2
4	0	7	3	6	0	3
8	6	9	4	7	1	1
5	6	3	8	0	1	1

69 BOX NUMBER

What number belongs in the box marked ?

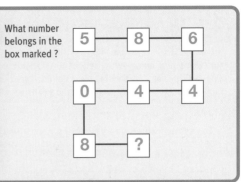

70 DOTTY DILEMMA

Connect adjacent dots with vertical or horizontal lines so that a single loop is formed with no crossings or branches. Each number indicates how many lines surround it, while empty cells may be surrounded by any number of lines.

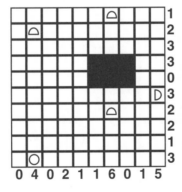

67 BATTLESHIPS

Do you remember the old game of battleships? This puzzle is based on that idea. Your task is to find the 10 vessels in the diagram. Some parts of boats or a sea square have already been filled in, and a number next to a row or column refers to the number of occupied squares in that row or column. A row or column with nothing next to it does not necessarily mean that there are no ship parts there. The boats may be positioned horizontally or vertically, but no two boats or parts of boats are in adjacent squares – horizontally, vertically or diagonally.

Shapes and numbers of ships to find:

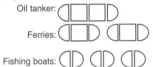

Oil tanker:
Ferries:
Fishing boats:
Yachts:

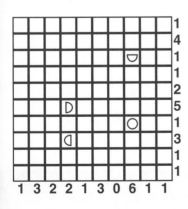

71 WIRED UP

Which of the four plugs is connected to the chainsaw?

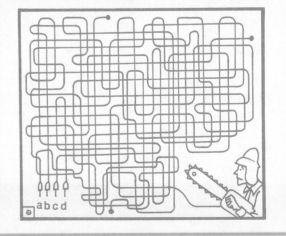

Shapes and numbers of ships to find:

Oil tanker:
Ferries:
Fishing boats:
Yachts:

72 COMMONWEALTH GAMES

●●● ○

Four house-sharing students from the University of Goatsferry's School of Medicine, finding themselves short of money on a cold, wet evening, decided to stay home and play a game – but they spent all their time arguing about which game they should play! From the clues given below, can you fill in on the drawing the name and country of origin of each student, and the game they wanted to play?

Clues

1　The student who wanted to play Monopoly was seated immediately clockwise of Rajendra Patel, who comes from India.

2　The Canadian student who wanted to play mah-jong wasn't Matt Scott.

3　The student from Barbados wasn't the one who wanted to play Trivial Pursuit, who wasn't in seat B.

4　The student in seat C wanted to play Scrabble.

5　Beverly McBain, who is not Australian, was in seat A.

Students: Beverly McBain; Jayne Bailey; Matt Scott; Rajendra Patel
Countries: Australia; Barbados; Canada; India
Games: mah-jong; Monopoly; Scrabble; Trivial Pursuit

Student: _____
Country: _____
Game: _____

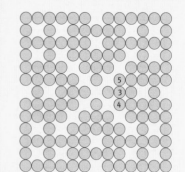

A

D

B

C

Student: _____
Country: _____
Game: _____

Starting tip: Work out which game student B wanted to play.

73 MASTERMIND BANDITS

●●●

The one-armed bandits in the puzzle-mad land of Enigmatica are different from those we might be familiar with in amusement arcades and on seaside piers. To play this version of the game, punters pull the handle and the four rollers spin and stop to reveal four fruits. The window next to the rollers then lights up to reveal how well that spin matches up with the jackpot line hidden by a shield at the bottom of the fruit machine. An X in the results window indicates that one roller is exactly correct, that is, a right fruit on the right roller. An O indicates that one fruit is correct in that it appears in the winning combination, but is on the wrong roller. Enigmaticans are given four pulls of the handle and then have to deduce the winning jackpot combination. Below is a machine at that final stage of the game after the four pulls of the handle. Can you emulate the good people of Enigmatica and work out the details of the winning line hidden beneath the jackpot shield?

Symbols:

Cherry

Orange

Lemon

Grapefruit

Banana

Pear

74 SUIT YOURSELF

●●●

Based on an idea by J. E. T. Thorne of Sanderstead

Four women recently enjoyed a bridge evening in the course of which they all had to defend their bids, some more boldly than others. From the clues given, can you indicate in the diagram each woman's position at the table and the number and suit of her bid?

Clues

1　Mrs Evans' bid was higher than that of the player on her left but one less than that of her partner; neither of them bid Diamonds, the one who did bidding one higher than the player at South.

2　Mrs Jennings was next left to the player whose suit was Hearts, but whose bid was not 6.

3　Mrs Scott's partner bid an odd number of No Trumps, while she her-self made an even-numbered bid though not in Spades.

4　Mrs Ryan neither played North nor made a bid of 5.

Players: Mrs Evans; Mrs Jennings; Mrs Ryan; Mrs Scott
Suits: Diamonds; Hearts; No Trumps; Spades
Bids: 3; 4; 5; 6

North　　　East

Player: _____
Suit: _____
Bid: _____

West　　　South

Player: _____
Suit: _____
Bid: _____

Starting tip: Narrow down the possibilities for the bids of Mrs Evans and her partner and then their seats.

75 NUMBER KROSS

○ ○ ○

See how quickly you can fit all these numbers into the grid. We've filled one number in to start you off.

3 figures			
110	1948	16422	82759	471017
228	2587	22212	85177	520293
342	3118	25719	92056	588289
534	4419	32023	96145	630580
618	6720	35081		640658
720	7732	49887	6 figures	731290
840	8313	50450	156414	772042
935	9821	54578	246647	834015
		63958	272674	897613
4 figures	5 figures	70598	309220	900510
	16334	76756	402631	913097

5
3
4

Travel from the entrance to the exit of the maze, filling the path completely to create a picture.

77 IT FIGURES

Place a number from 1 to 9 in each empty cell so that the sum of each vertical or horizontal block equals the number at the top or on the left of that block. Numbers may only be used once in each block.

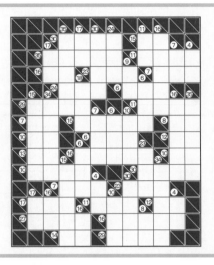

78 COLOUR CHAOS

The day after Dreadnought Bathroom Supplies Ltd had held their annual dinner-dance, six enraged customers phoned to complain that the six supposedly matching elements of their new bathroom suites had in fact been delivered in six different colours: avocado, dove, lemon, mango, peach and rose.

At 9.35am, Fenella, the DBS receptionist, contemplated the full complaints sheet and hoped that she would remain undisturbed until home time. The calls had started at 9.05am and had come at five-minute intervals. She noticed that in some consecutive boxes on her sheet the initial letters of the colours spelt out words.

The Soap family had PAR in their row of colours and the same word also appeared in a column. The Faucett family had LAD in their row and the Lathers had PAD. There was LAMP reading somewhere down the shower-tray column and LAP was to be seen in another column. The Waters family phoned some time after the Soaps, but fifteen minutes before the Lather household. The Tubbs family had been sent a lemon bath and they phoned some time before the Faucetts and some time after the Flannell family. The peach bidet was noted ten minutes after the rose cistern, but ten minutes before the mango basin. The dove lavatory was noted ten minutes after the peach basin, but ten minutes before the avocado bath. Can you complete Fenella's complaints sheet?

Time	Customer	Basin	Bath	Bidet	Cistern	Lavatory	Shower
9.05							
9.10							
9.15							
9.20							
9.25							
9.30							

80 TWINNED-UP

This boy would like to buy a spinning top identical to the one he's holding. Which one will he choose?

79 CYCLE OF MISHAPS

The diagram shows the cross section of a difficult stage of an international cycle race, during which various riders had to drop out at the points marked 1 to 7. From the clues given below, can you name the rider who dropped out at each position, and pinpoint the reason for his withdrawal from the race?

Clues

1 One rider's pedal snapped due to metal fatigue; this was two points beyond the one where Dirk had to drop out.

2 The name of the rider who withdrew at point 6 appears in the alphabetical list immediately before that of the one whose chain broke.

3 Roland dropped out next but one before the rider whose wheel became buckled.

4 It was at point 3 that one injury-prone rider twisted his ankle.

5 Yves' flat tyre caused him to withdraw at an even-numbered location.

6 Michel was obliged to abandon the race at point 4 on the plan.

7 The rider at point 5 has a longer name than the man whose suspect knee gave way, who was not Bjorn.

8 Victor was not the rider who suffered a disabling attack of migraine during the race.

Riders: Bjorn; Dirk; Gino; Michel; Roland; Victor; Yves
Reasons for withdrawal: buckled wheel; chain broke; flat tyre; knee gave way; migraine attack; pedal snapped; twisted ankle

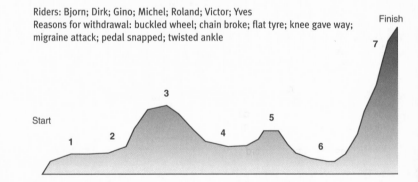

Rider: ___ ___ ___ ___ ___ ___ ___

Reason: ___ ___ ___ ___ ___ ___ ___

Starting tip: Begin by working out at which point Yves had to drop out.

81 ACE IN PLACE

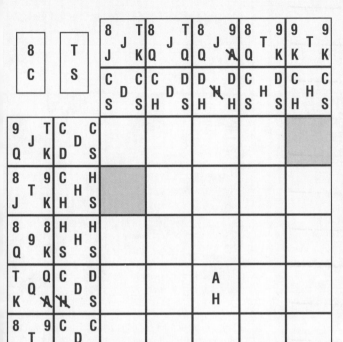

The cards Eight to King of each suit, together with the Ace of Hearts have been placed in a 5 x 5 square. Figures and letters showing the values 8, 9, 10, J, Q, K and suits C, H, D, S have been placed at the end of each line across and down. With the Ace in place and the fact that the two cards shown at the top left belong in the shaded squares, can you work out the unique place for each card?

85 ARMS AND THE MAN

Four hereditary peers own the coats of arms featured in the diagram. From the clues given below, can you name the owner of each of the shields lettered A to D, say which heraldic device appears on each, and work out the background colour of each coat of arms?

Clues

1 Lord Rackham's shield features a turkey, in cryptic reference to one of his remote ancestors' heroic deeds in that land against the infidel during the Crusades; it is somewhere to the left of the blue coat of arms.

2 The yellow shield is somewhere to the right of the one depicting an eagle, which can be seen alongside Lord Bertram's arms in the diagram.

3 The lion does not feature on Lord Mallender's coat of arms.

4 The background colour of shield C is green.

5 Shield A is the coat of arms of Lord Liversedge.

Peers: Lord Bertram; Lord Liversedge; Lord Mallender; Lord Rackham
Devices: eagle; lion; stag; turkey
Colours: blue; green; red; yellow

A   **B**   **C**   **D**

Peer: _____ _____ _____ _____
Device: _____ _____ _____ _____
Colour: _____ _____ _____ _____

Starting tip: Begin by working out the colour of shield A.

82 POSER

The artist has made five mistakes while trying to paint an exact portrait of the model. Can you spot the five errors?

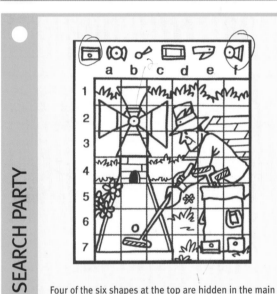

83 SEARCH PARTY

Four of the six shapes at the top are hidden in the main picture. Can you work out which ones and whereabouts they appear?

84 CODE MASTER

Just follow the rules of that classic puzzle, Master Mind, to crack the colour code. The first number tells you how many of the pegs are exactly correct – the right colour in the right place (✓✓). The second number tells you how many pegs are the correct colour but are not in the right place (✓). Colours may be repeated in the answer. By comparing the information given by each line, can you work out which colour goes in which place?

				✓✓	✓
●	●	●	●	2	0
●	●	●	●	0	2
●	●	●	●	0	1
●	●	●	●	0	0
●	●	●	●	1	2
○	○	○	○	4	0

86 TWIN SET

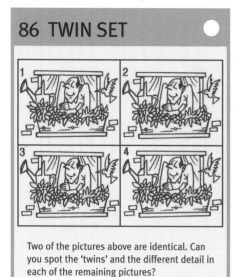

Two of the pictures above are identical. Can you spot the 'twins' and the different detail in each of the remaining pictures?

87 FOURSOME

This woman would like to buy four identical vases. Which design will she choose?

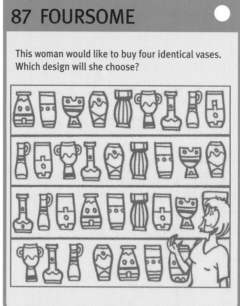

88 IT FIGURES

Place a number from 1 to 9 in each empty cell so that the sum of each vertical or horizontal block equals the number at the top or on the left of that block. Numbers may only be used once in each block.

89 DOT-TO-DOT

Join the dots from 1 to 40 to reveal the hidden picture.

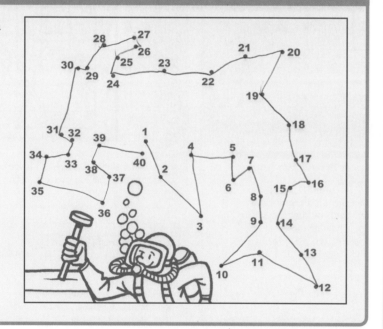

90 SILHOUETTE

Shade in every fragment containing a dot – and what have you got?

91 CODE MASTER

Just follow the rules of that classic puzzle, Master Mind, to crack the colour code. The first number tells you how many of the pegs are exactly correct – the right colour in the right place (✓✓) The second number tells you how many pegs are the correct colour but are not in the right place (✓). Colours may be repeated in the answer. By comparing the information given by each line, can you work out which colour goes in which place?

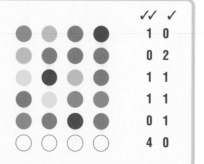

	✓✓	✓
	1	0
	0	2
	1	1
	1	1
	0	1
	4	0

92 DOTTY DILEMMA ●●●

Connect adjacent dots with vertical or horizontal lines so that a single loop is formed with no crossings or branches. Each number indicates how many lines surround it, while empty cells may be surrounded by any number of lines.

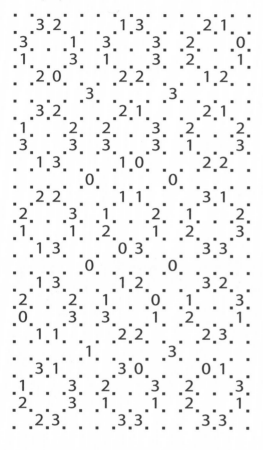

93 BATTLESHIPS ●●●

Do you remember the old game of battleships? These puzzles are based on that idea. Your task is to find the vessels in the diagram. Some parts of boats or sea squares have already been filled in, and a number next to a row or column refers to the number of occupied squares in that row or column. The boats may be positioned horizontally or vertically, but no two boats or parts of boats are in adjacent squares – horizontally, vertically or diagonally.

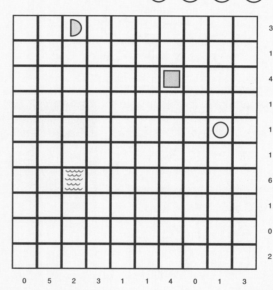

Aircraft carrier:

Battleships:

Cruisers:

Destroyers:

94 KEEPING IN TOUCH

Diana was an inveterate letter-writer, keeping in touch with all her former school friends by post on a regular basis. The other day she wrote four letters to friends in different parts of the country. From the clues given below, can you fill in the full names and the town which appeared on each envelope lying on the table in the positions numbered 1 to 4?

Clues

1 Betty's letter is immediately to the right of the one addressed to Mrs Hardy.

2 Letter 2 is about to wing its way to Nantwich; it is not the one addressed to Mrs Riley.

3 Jenny's name appears on the envelope containing letter 3; she does not live in Hull.

4 The letter to Cardiff is somewhere to the left on the table of the one addressed to Sally.

5 Mrs Dukes is destined to receive letter 1.

First names: Betty; Jenny; Jill; Sally
Surnames: Dukes; Hardy; Markham; Riley
Towns: Cardiff; Hull; Ipswich; Nantwich

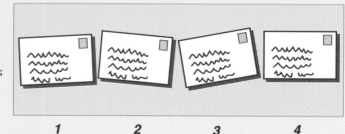

First name: _____ _____ _____ _____
Surname: _____ _____ _____ _____
Town: _____ _____ _____ _____

Starting tip: Start by working out which letter is addressed to Mrs Hardy.

95 SILHOUETTE

Shade in every fragment containing a dot – and what have you got?

96 TRILINES

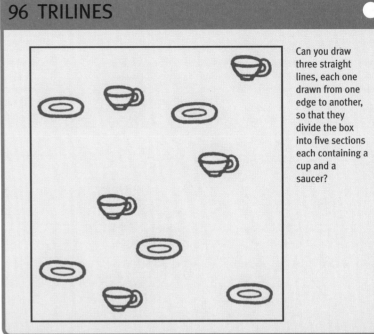

Can you draw three straight lines, each one drawn from one edge to another, so that they divide the box into five sections each containing a cup and a saucer?

97 SNAPSHOT

Can you work out which of nine photographs is an exact replica of the model?

98 MARKING THE CHANGES

Mr Prendergast, who teaches maths at Netherlipp High, always has four coloured pens in his top pocket. A pupil, whose mind kept drifting away from considering the implications of Pythagoras, noticed that each day this week up to Thursday no pen stayed in the same position. His observations are embodied in the clues which should enable you to work out the position of each pen on each day.

Clues

Colours: black; blue; green; red

1 On Monday the blue was next left to the red but on Thursday the red was next left to the blue.

2 The green was in the same place on Monday as the red on Wednesday and in the same place on Tuesday as the black on Wednesday.

3 The green was one place further left on Wednesday than on Tuesday and one place further left on Thursday than on Monday.

4 On Tuesday the red was third from the left.

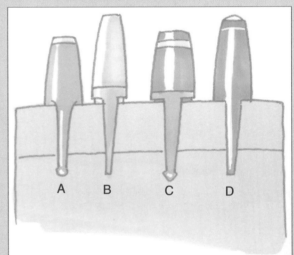

Monday: _____

Tuesday: _____

Wednesday: _____

Thursday: _____

Starting tip: Work out the colour of pen D on Thursday.

99 BAKE ME A CAKE

The cake stall is always popular at the monthly church fund-raising event. This month the four cakes at the front of the stall, numbered 1 to 4 in the diagram, were sold within seconds of the opening. From the clues given below, can you describe each cake, and name the woman who made it and the one who bought it?

Clues

1 Thelma bought the cake made by Mary, which was immediately to the right of the chocolate cake on the table.

2 Betty did not make the fruit cake, which was not bought by Linda, and Jean's cake was not number 4.

3 Cake 2 was made by Eileen.

4 The ginger sponge cake was in position 3 on the stall.

5 The jelly sponge was next but one on the table to the cake bought by Hilary.

Cakes: chocolate; ginger sponge; fruit cake; jelly sponge
Cake bakers: Betty; Eileen; Jean; Mary
Buyers: Hilary; Linda; Sarah; Thelma

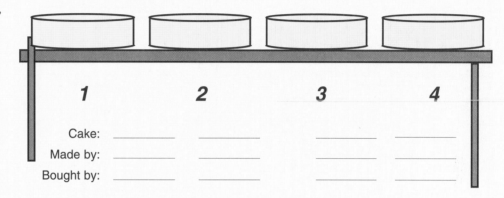

Cake: _____ _____ _____ _____

Made by: _____ _____ _____ _____

Bought by: _____ _____ _____ _____

Starting tip: Start by numbering the chocolate cake.

100 STRICTLY FOR THE BIRDS

The women in four neighbouring semi-detached houses each cooked a different bird for their family's Christmas dinner, though all followed it up with the traditional Christmas pudding. From the clues given below, can you identify the cook at each of the houses numbered 6 to 12, and say which bird her family dined on?

Women: Beryl; Denise; Elaine; Molly
Surnames: Bird; Carver; Fowler; Legge
Birds: chicken; duck; goose; turkey

Clues

1 Denise Carver's house is the other half of the one where the duck was cooked.

2 The Fowler family dined on turkey, but not at number 8.

3 The Birds live at number 6; the woman who cooked their dinner is not Elaine.

4 Beryl lives at a house numbered two higher than the one where the family enjoyed a goose for their Christmas dinner.

5 The traditionalists at number 10 ate their usual chicken at dinner-time on Christmas Day.

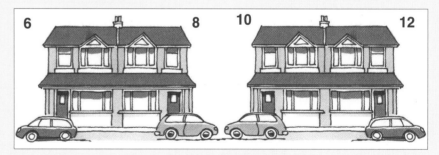

Woman: _____ _____

Surname: _____ _____

Bird: _____ _____

Starting tip: Start by working out the first name of Mrs Bird.

101 MAZE MYSTERY

Travel from the entrance to the exit of the maze, filling the path completely to create a picture.

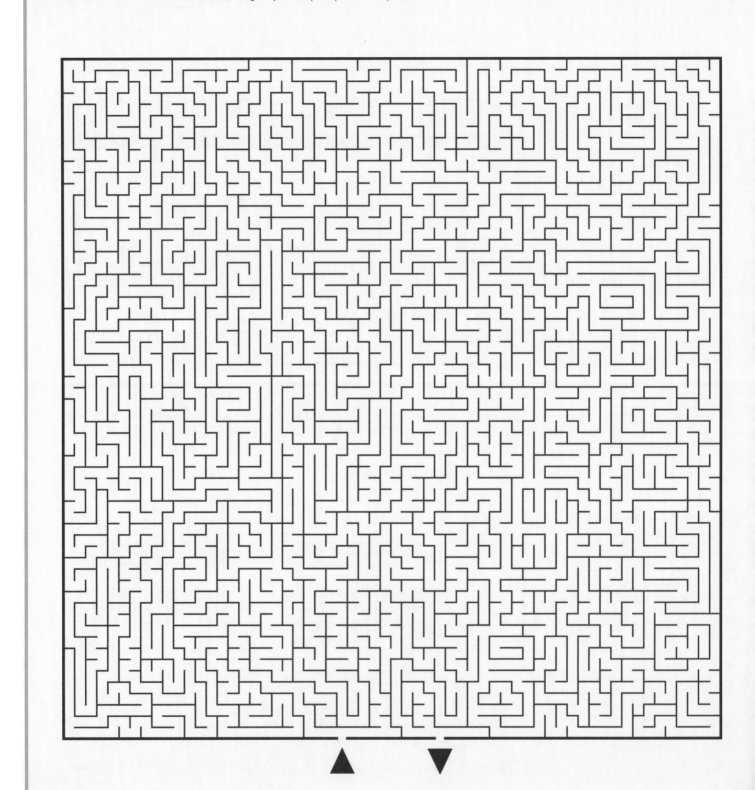

102 LITTLE AND LARGE

In this puzzle, the little numbers are large and the large numbers are little! Each little number from 1 to 9 is to be placed into the boxes, one per box.

Each larger number in the boxes is the sum of the little number that goes in it plus the little number in each box with which it shares an edge.

So the corner squares have two neighbours, the rest along the sides, three and the square in the middle has four. From the little larger numbers given, and the large little numbers already placed, can you fill in the rest?

14 **3**	16	15
24	29	21
16	21	15 **4**

103 CODE MASTER

Just follow the rules of that classic puzzle, Master Mind, to crack the colour code. The first number tells you how many of the pegs are exactly correct – the right colour in the right place (✓✓).

The second number tells you how many pegs are the correct colour but are not in the right place (✓). Colours may be repeated in the answer.

By comparing the information given by each line, can you work out which colour goes in which place?

	✓✓	✓
● ● ● ●	1	1
● ● ● ●	2	0
● ● ● ●	1	1
● ● ● ●	2	1
● ● ● ●	0	2
○ ○ ○ ○	4	0

104 WHAT'S YOUR GAME?

Andy Player is giving board games to all his friends this Christmas and at the moment the parcels are stacked up in the corner of his living room as shown in the drawing. From the clues given below, can you work out who each parcel is addressed to, and which game is in it?

Clues

1 The Longs' present is immediately below the one intended for the Dixons.
2 Parcel E contains the game Andy's giving John and Laura Smith.
3 The *Advantage* game is in contact with just one other present, the one meant for the Woods.
4 The present addressed to Mike and Fran Brown is immediately above the *Terminator* game and immediately below the backgammon set; the latter is not next

but one in the stack to the Fields' present.
5 The *X-Words* game which Andy has bought for Frank and Carol Allen is not at the bottom of the pile.
6 The elaborate Roman-style chess set, which is not parcel G, is between the presents Andy is giving to the Fields and to the Kings, neither of which is next to the parcel addressed to the Smiths.
7 Parcel C contains the game *Stonewall*; the *Hippodrome* horse-racing game isn't in parcel F.

Presents for: Allens; Browns; Dixons; Fields; Kings; Longs; Smiths; Woods
Games: *Advantage*; backgammon; chess; *Grand Tour*; *Hippodrome*; *Stonewall*; *Terminator*; *X-Words*

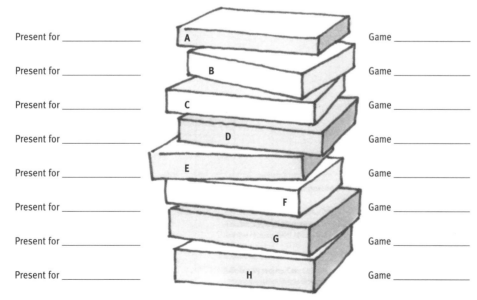

Present for _____ A   Game _____
Present for _____ B   Game _____
Present for _____ C   Game _____
Present for _____ D   Game _____
Present for _____ E   Game _____
Present for _____ F   Game _____
Present for _____ G   Game _____
Present for _____ H   Game _____

Starting tip: Work out for whom present H is intended.

105 MATCH BLOCKS

There are three identical squares in the grid below. Can you spot them? Watch out though, they may not be the same way up!

106 BATTLE GROUND

Each figure features one detail that is not present in the other three. Can you spot all four extra details?

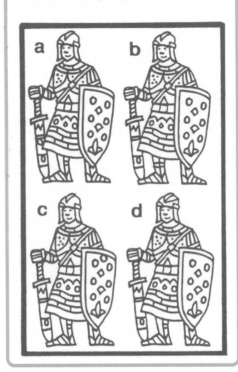

107 SCATTER-PILLAR

Can you rearrange the six fragments below to form two identical pillars?

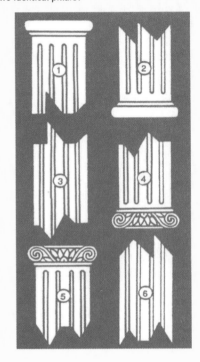

108 SQUARE NUMBERS

The digits, ranging from 1 to 9, in each of the five lines and columns in this square add up to 23; three have been inserted. From the clues given below, can you fill in the rest?

CLUES
1 In every line there are three odd and two even digits, as there are also in columns 1, 3 and 4; column 2 has four even and column 5 five odd digits. There are no repeated digits in any line, but column 1 has a repeated odd digit, like column 5; the other columns have no repeated digits.
2 The two 9s are in lines 1 and 4, the two 8s are in two other successive lines and the two lines which contain a 7 have a line separating them; the three 1s are in successive lines and the three 2s are in odd-numbered lines; only in line 3 is there no 3 and only in line 4 is there no 5; there are no 5s in columns 1 and 2.
3 In lines 2 and 3 the highest digit immediately precedes the lowest but in line 4 the lowest immediately precedes the highest. In line 1 the second digit is one higher than the fourth, but in line 5 the second is lower than the fourth.
4 The square at the intersection of line 3 and column 4 does not contain 5; the square at the end of line 3 contains an odd digit.

Starting tip: Work out in which lines the 8s appear.

	1	2	3	4	5
1					5
2					
3					
4					
5	3				5

109 LITTLE AND LARGE

In this puzzle, the little numbers are large and the large numbers are little! Each little number from 1 to 9 is to be placed into the boxes, one per box. Each larger number in the boxes is the sum of the little number that goes in it plus the little number in each box with which it shares an edge.

So the corner squares have two neighbours, the rest along the sides, three and the square in the middle has four. From the little larger numbers given, and the large little numbers already placed, can you fill in the rest?

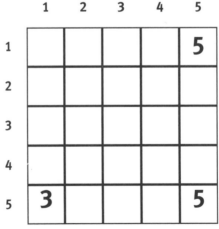

38

110 ISLAND HOPPING

Each circle containing a number represents an island. The object is to connect each island with vertical or horizontal bridges so that:
* The number of bridges is the same as the number inside the island.
* There can be up to two bridges between two islands.
* Bridges cannot cross islands or other bridges.
* There is a continuous path connecting all the islands.

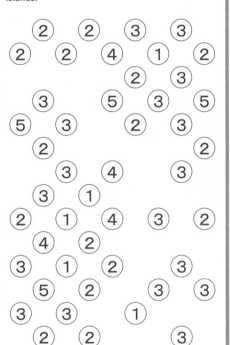

111 DOT-TO-DOT

Join the dots from 1 to 38 to reveal the hidden picture.

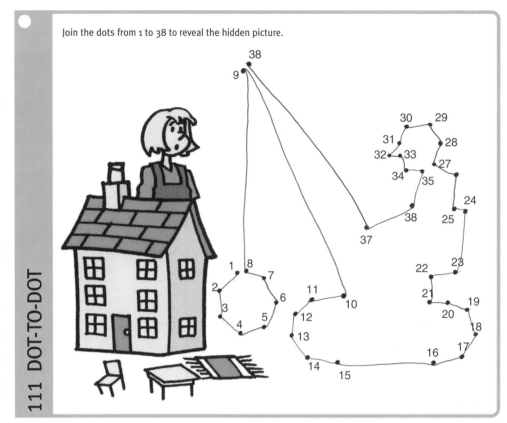

114 DIGIT FIDGET

The 10 digits are rewritten so that none is in its correct position, counting, 0–9 from the left.

1 is two places right of 0,
5 two places right of 4,
2 two places right of 8,
9 two places right of 7,
6 three left of 2,
4 three left of 3.

Can you rewrite the number?

113 MIRROR IMAGE

Can you work out which reflection belongs to each of the hat wearers, Andy, Ben and Colin, who are shown at the top?

112 STRIP TRICK

Can you arrange the numbered strips in order to create the coiled strip shown at the top?

115 NUMBER KROSS

See how quickly you can fit all these numbers into the grid. We've filled one number in to start you off.

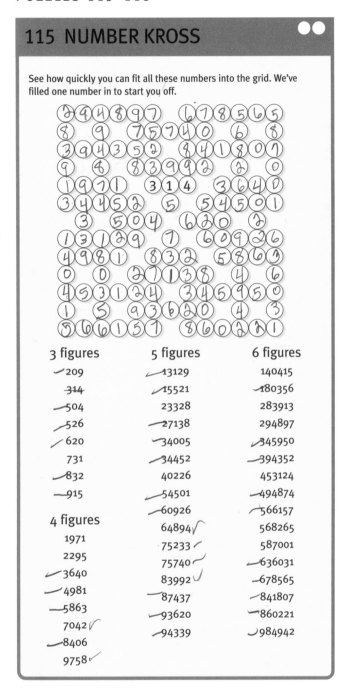

3 figures	5 figures	6 figures
209	13129	140415
314	15521	180356
504	23328	283913
526	27138	294897
620	34005	345950
731	34452	394352
832	40226	453124
915	54501	494874
	60926	566157
4 figures	64894	568265
1971	75233	587001
2295	75740	636031
3640	83992	678565
4981	87437	841807
5863	93620	860221
7042	94339	984942
8406		
9758		

116 SAFE BET

This is an odd safe. Solve all the clues and find the combination in the shaded squares.

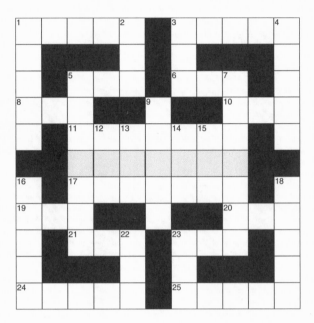

ACROSS

1 Subtract 68,017 from *4 down*
3 Half of *1 across*
5 Twice *3 down*
6 First three digits of *25 across*
8 Next in series 595, 664, 733,…, then add 40
10 Subtract 204 from *22 down*
11 Square first four digits of *1 across*
17 Add 567,971 to *11 across*
19 Last three digits of *17 across*
20 Reverse digits of *23 across*
21 Square root of 259,081
23 Add 300 to *21 across*
24 Subtract 30 squared from *6 across* squared, then add 40
25 3 per cent of 410,700

DOWN

1 Add *3 across* to *24 across*
2 Subtract 40 from *8 across*
3 Square root of *25 across*
4 Add 82,986 to *24 across*
5 Subtract 1,511,194 from *7 down*
7 Add 3,780,988 to *9 down*
9 Subtract 5,000 from *18 down*
12 Add 90 to *13 down*
13 Subtract 96,834 from *4 down*
14 Subtract 10 from *22 down*
15 Square root of 40,000
16 Add 1,000 to *18 down*
18 3 per cent of 603,700
22 Multiply *3 down* by 9
23 Subtract 99 from *19 across*

118 SCOOP

At Justa Conesa Italian ice cream parlour, combinations of cones, scoops and chocolate bars are charged per item:

Chocca Likka –
1 cone, 1 scoop, 2 chocolate bars 80 cents
Coola Cona –
1 cone, 2 scoops, 1 chocolate bar 95 cents
Plain –
1 cone, 1 scoop 40 cents
From this – can you work out the cost of one scoop of ice cream?

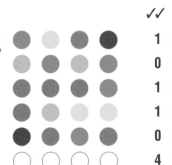

117 CODE MASTER

Just follow the rules of that classic puzzle, Master Mind, to crack the colour code. The first number tells you how many of the pegs are exactly correct – the right colour in the right place (✓✓). The second number tells you how many pegs are the correct colour but are not in the right place (✓). Colours may be repeated in the answer. By comparing the information given by each line, can you work out which colour goes in which place?

				✓✓	✓
				1	0
				0	1
				1	0
				1	0
				0	0
				4	0

119 TWOS AND THREES

Which of the articles below appear four times?

120 IT FIGURES

Place a number from 1 to 9 in each empty cell so that the sum of each vertical or horizontal block equals the number at the top or on the left of that block. Numbers may only be used once in each block.

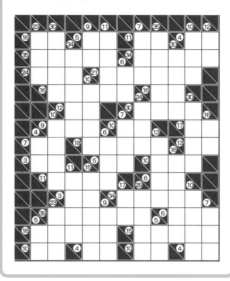

121 NUMBER SQUARES

Can you complete the grids with the aid of the numbers given, so that all sums, whether horizontal or vertical, are correct? (Please note that each sum should be treated separately.)

122 THIRTY DAYS HATH NOVEMBER

Each of the thirty days of November is inscribed in a different box in the diagram. From the clues given below, can you insert the correct date in each of the boxes?

Clues

1 The 15th, 23rd and 4th of the month are in consecutive boxes reading from left to right in the same horizontal row.

2 The 1st is in box C3; the only other single-digit date in row C is its immediate left-hand neighbour, and there are no more such dates at all in column 3.

3 The 11th is in the box immediately below the 21st, and the 24th is diagonally adjacent, below right, to the 22nd.

4 Box B4 contains a date five days after the one in A2.

5 The 30th is immediately below the 28th.

6 The 3rd, the 20th and the 9th are, reading from top to bottom, in the top three boxes of one vertical column.

7 The two days which immediately follow the one in B2 are, respectively, in D6 and D3.

8 Box A6 contains a two-digit even-numbered date, which is half the one to be found in C5.

9 One horizontal row begins with the 6th and ends with the 25th.

10 The 26th is two boxes above the 7th in the same column.

11 The 2nd, which has the 16th immediately to its left, is in the row above the 5th, which is two boxes right of the 13th, which is in the same vertical column as the 29th.

12 The 17th is somewhere in column 1, the 27th in column 2, and the 19th somewhere in row B.

13 The 10th is in a higher row than the 12th, but not in the same column.

Dates:

1	2	3	4
5	6	7	8
9	10	11	12
13	14	15	16
17	18	19	20
21	22	23	24
25	26	27	28
29	30		

Starting tip: Begin by placing the 9th in its correct box.

	1	2	3	4	5	6
A						
B						
C						
D						
E						

123 LUDO ●●●

Four little girls sat down one rainy day to play a traditional game of ludo. From the clues given below, can you say who sat in each of positions 1 to 4, decide which colour of counters each had chosen for the game, and work out what number of spots on the dice each had obtained with her most recent throw?

Clues

1 No player had a number of spots on the dice which corresponded with the number indicating her position at the table.

2 Rachel, who threw a three, was next clockwise from the player using the yellow counters.

3 The red counters on the board belonged to Theresa.

4 The player in seat 2 had just thrown a six.

5 It was a blue counter which was moved four squares after one player's last throw; this was not Angela.

6 Yvonne was not sitting in seat 3.

Names: Angela; Rachel; Theresa; Yvonne
Counters: blue; green; red; yellow
Spots on dice: 1; 3; 4; 6

Name: _____
Counters: _____   1
Spots: _____

Name: _____   4
Counters: _____
Spots: _____

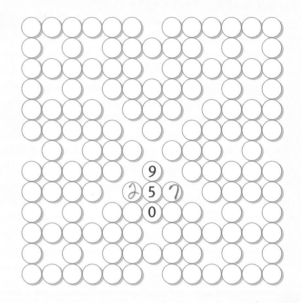

2
_____
_____
_____

3
Name: _____
Counters: _____
Spots: _____

Starting tip: Start by working out the colour of Rachel's counters.

124 NUMBER KROSS ●●

See how quickly you can fit all these numbers into the grid. We've filled one number in to start you off.

9
2 5 7
0

3 figures	5 figures	6 figures
147	14214	101723
~~257~~	17012	107028
348	21234	201034
439	27893	279469
527	30514	304050
731	39130	317029
823	43297	417924
~~950~~	50781	450353
	54829	557894
4 figures	69483	575859
1735	71335	610778
2007	71827	721707
3976	80724	771644
4041	82133	809010
5923	93009	817345
6125	94345	971872
7409		
8422		

125 DOT-TO-DOT

Join the dots from 1 to 45 to reveal the hidden picture.

126 FIGURE IT OUT

Each digit from 1–9 appears four times in the square, no similar digits being diagonally adjacent. Where the same digit appears more than once in any row or column, this is stated. Can you complete the square?

Row
1 Two 4s and two 9s; total 34
2 One even, two odd, two even, one odd digit from left to right; lowest is 2; total 37
3 Two 1s separated by an 8; two 5s but no 4s
4 Two adjacent 6s with an odd digit and two 8s
5 Two 3s separated by a 6; highest is a 7; total 22
6 Two adjacent 7s; total 24

Column
1 Two 8s separated by an odd digit; total 29
2 Two adjacent 9s; the other digits also total 18
3 Two adjacent 2s; total 27
4 Two 9s separated by two digits; total 31
5 Two 6s separated by two digits, all bracketed by two odd digits
6 Total 22

	1	2	3	4	5	6
1						
2						
3						
4						
5						
6						

127 ON SITE

Four couples are having a holiday in their caravans on a popular seaside site. From the clues given below, can you name the couple in each of the caravans numbered 1 to 4, and say where each pair is from?

Clues
1 Paul's caravan is somewhere to the right of the one being used by Alicia, from Cardiff, and her partner.
2 Esme and her partner are separated from Desmond and his partner only by the couple from Belfast.
3 Sebastian and Zoe have a lower-numbered caravan than the couple from London.
4 Miranda is staying in caravan 3, but not with Luther.

Males: Desmond; Luther; Paul; Sebastian
Females: Alicia; Esme; Miranda; Zoe
Cities: Belfast; Cardiff; Edinburgh; London

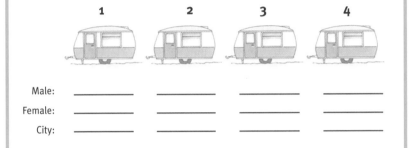

Male: _____ _____ _____ _____
Female: _____ _____ _____ _____
City: _____ _____ _____ _____

Starting tip: Start by naming the woman in caravan 4.

128 NUMBER TREE

Sixteen leaves are on the eight branches of the tree and each contains a different number from 1 to 16. Using the following clues, can you determine which number is on which leaf? All the totals of two leaves at the same height are different (leaf 2 is at the same height as leaf 9, 3 is the same as 10 and so on). Four of the totals of the leaves on each branch are unique but the other two totals each appear twice. No number is the same as the leaf that it is on and no two consecutive numbers are on the same branch or at the same height. The seven prime numbers, including 1, are all on leaves which have prime numbers. 2 and 14 are on the same branch and the number on leaf 14 is a multiple of that on 12. A leaf containing a square number is immediately above another with a square number, neither of the square numbers being 9. Number 7 is higher than number 9 which is higher than number 10, which is immediately below number 1. The total of leaf 9 (which does not contain 15) and leaf 11 is the same as the total of the numbers on leaves 5 and 7. Number 13 is at the same height as number 4 which is somewhere higher than number 16. Number 1 is immediately below an odd number. Only two branches contain two odd numbers and the total of the numbers on leaves 6 and 8 is a prime number, which is also the same as the total of one of the branches. Number 3 is somewhere below number 11.

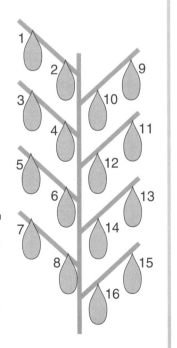

129 TWINNED UP

The twins would like to buy matching belts. Which two will they choose?

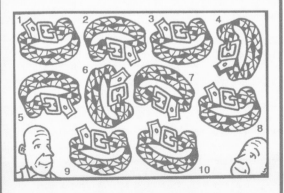

130 MODERN ART

Having bought one of the abstract paintings, the art-lover can't remember which one it is or which way up it should go. Can you help him?

131 CODE MASTER

Just follow the rules of that classic puzzle, Master Mind, to crack the colour code. The first number tells you how many of the pegs are exactly correct – the right colour in the right place (✓✓). The second number tells you how many pegs are the correct colour but are not in the right place (✓). Colours may be repeated in the answer. By comparing the information given by each line, can you work out which colour goes in which place?

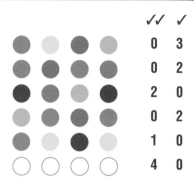

✓✓	✓
0	3
0	2
2	0
0	2
1	0
4	0

132 MATCH-BLOCKS

Can you spot which three squares in the picture below are identical? Watch out, though – they may not be the same way up!

133 CROSS-SUMS

With the help of the number already in place in the grid, see if you can fill in the cell, using the numbers listed below. The rule which decides what goes where is that the number in the top square of each cross of five squares must equal the total of the numbers in the square of that cross for instance

X+A=B=C=D

1	2	3	4	5	6	7
8	9	10	11	12	31	48
51	51	61	74	109	121	181
~~399~~	427	462	1469			

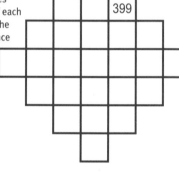

134 SQUARE NUMBERS

The numbers 1–25 are entered randomly in a 5 x 5 square so that no two consecutive numbers are adjacent in any direction, or included in any row, column or long diagonal. The four corner numbers are all two-digit prime numbers increasing each time clockwise starting from one of the corners. E4 is twice that in C1 but only half B3. D5 is twice C5 but only half A2. A4 is twice D3 but only half B2. B1 and D4 are both prime, the latter being five higher than D5; C1 and C4 total 25; E2 plus E3 equals C1, the former being less than the latter. B1 plus B5 equals D2. Can you locate each number?

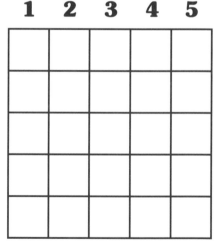

135 IN THE LOCKER ROOM

●●●

The diagram shows a block of lockers in the men's changing room at the squash club. From the clues given below, can you fully identify and describe the men who are currently using each of the lockers numbered 1 to 4?

Clues

1 The priest is using the locker immediately above Melvin's.
2 Denzil's locker is the one immediately to the right of Fettle's.
3 The bank manager is using locker number 4.
4 Gareth's locker is in diagonal alignment with the one the lecturer is using.
5 Kieron's locker is on the same level as the lawyer's.
6 Spry's locker has a number one lower than Hardy's.

First names: Denzil; Gareth; Kieron; Melvin
Surnames: Fettle; Fitt; Hardy; Spry
Descriptions: bank manager; priest; lawyer; lecturer

Starting tip: Begin by working out the first name of the man using locker 1.

First name: _____ _____
Surname: _____ _____
Description: _____ _____

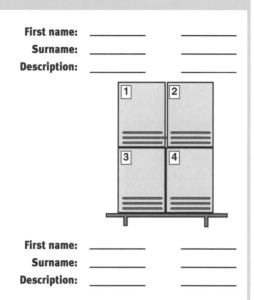

First name: _____ _____
Surname: _____ _____
Description: _____ _____

136 SUDOKU

●●●

Place a number from 1 to 9 in each empty cell so that each row, each column and each 3 x 3 block contains all the numbers from 1 to 9.

						5	6	4
	1	2	9					
		3		8				
		6						3
	2		6		5		7	
7						8		
			4		1			
				7	6	9		
2	5	8						

137 BATTLESHIPS

●●●

Do you remember the old game of battleships? These puzzles are based on that idea. Your task is to find the vessels in the diagram. Some parts of boats or sea squares have already been filled in, and a number next to a row or column refers to the number of occupied squares in that row or column. The boats may be positioned horizontally or vertically, but no two boats or parts of boats are in adjacent squares – horizontally, vertically or diagonally.

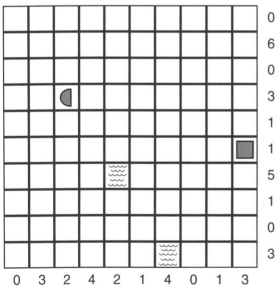

Row totals (top to bottom): 0, 6, 0, 3, 1, 1, 5, 1, 0, 3
Column totals (left to right): 0, 3, 2, 4, 2, 1, 4, 0, 1, 3

Aircraft carrier:
Battleships:
Cruisers:
Destroyers:

138 COSTUME DRAMA

●

Each picture contains a detail that is not present in the other three. Can you spot all four extra details?

139 ALL SQUARE

Each of the 16 small squares making up the large square in the diagram contains either one of the numbers 1 to 8 or the square of one of these numbers. From the clues given below, can you place the correct number in each square? NB The numbers 1 and 4 will, of course, each appear twice.

Clues

1 The numbers in the four corner squares, which are all different, total 21 when added together.
2 16 is immediately to the right of 64, and immediately below 49.
3 The 9 and 6 are both in column A.
4 Squares B2 and C4 both contain single-digit numbers, the former being an even number.
5 The total of the four numbers in row 1 is one higher than the number in square A2.
6 The number in square D2 is twice the one in C1.
7 The number in square B3 is the square of the one in D1.
8 The 25 and the 8 are on the same horizontal row of squares.
9 One of the 1s is in column B.
10 The number in C4 is the square root of one of the other numbers in column C.

Numbers: 1; 1; 2; 3; 4; 4; 5; 6; 7; 8; 9; 16; 25; 36; 49; 64

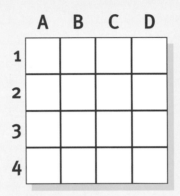

Starting tip: Begin by working out where to put the 16.

140 SILHOUETTE

Shade in every fragment containing a dot – and what have you got?

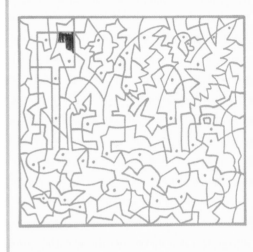

141 IT FIGURES

Place a number from 1 to 9 in each empty cell so that the sum of each vertical or horizontal block equals the number at the top or on the left of that block. Numbers may only be used once in each block.

142 SALLY'S GUESTS

Young Sally was allowed to invite three of her friends who live in the same street to stay at her house for lunch. At the end of the meal, each child was asked to choose which flavour of yoghurt she would like. From the clues given below, can you work out who sat in which position at the table, say at which number in the street she lives, and name her chosen yoghurt flavour?

Clues

1 The meal was served at an odd-numbered house.
2 Sally sat directly opposite Jenny, who chose cherry as her yoghurt flavour.
3 The strawberry yoghurt was consumed by the girl on chair number 3, whose home is not at number 11.
4 The girl on chair 4 lives at number 20.
5 The peach yoghurt was eaten by the girl who lives at number 15, whose counterclockwise neighbour at the table was Rosie.
6 Helen was not sitting in position 2.

Names: Helen; Jenny; Rosie; Sally
House numbers: 8; 11; 15; 20
Flavours: cherry; peach; pineapple; strawberry

Name: _____
House no.: _____
Flavour: _____

Name: _____
House no.: _____
Flavour: _____

Starting tip: First work out who was sitting on chair 2.

143 MAZE MYSTERY

Travel from the entrance to the exit of the maze, filling the path completely to create a picture.

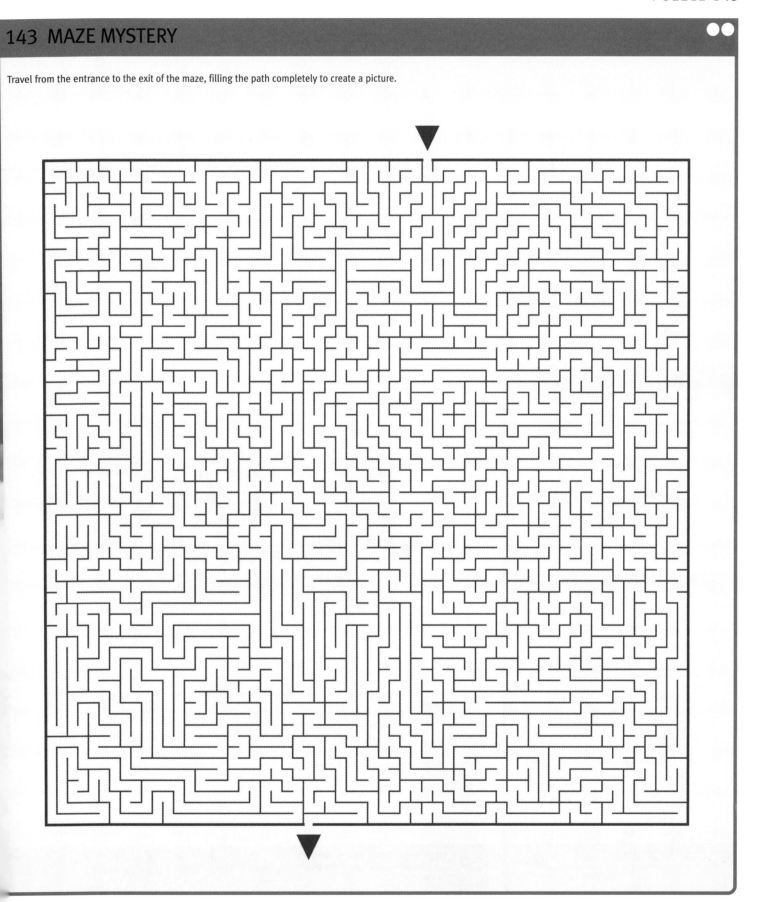

144 SILHOUETTE

Shade in every fragment containing a dot – and what have you got?

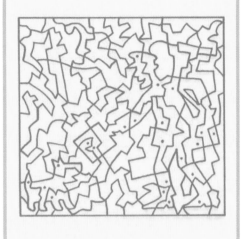

146 SUM-UP

Calculate the price of each pawn, castle, knight and king using the given totals.

145 TROPHIES

Karen Mills is 17, and a talented athlete. On the mantelpiece of her parents' home are displayed the three trophies which she's won this year. From the clues below, can you fill in on the diagram the details of each trophy: her placing, the event, the competition, and the month?

Clues

1 The 1,500 metres trophy was won the month after she received the third-place award, which isn't Trophy A.
2 Her discus trophy stands to the left of the one she won in July.
3 Trophy B was won at the County Amateur Athletics Association meeting, for a placing one higher than she achieved in the high jump.
4 It was in the annual town sports that she took a first place.

Placings: First; Second; Third
Events: Discus; 1,500 metres; high jump
Meetings: County; inter-schools; town
Months: May; June; July

Starting tip: Work out for which place Trophy B was awarded.

Placing:	_____	_____	_____
Event:	_____	_____	_____
Meeting:	_____	_____	_____
Month:	_____	_____	_____

A   B   C

147 TROUBLESOME TRIANGLE

The numbers 1–15 are to be inserted into the grid. No two consecutive numbers are in the same row or arrowed diagonal. The numbers on the left show the total in the horizontal row and those below show the total of the diagonal.

If squares 5 and 8 total 16, and in the diagonal totalling 27 only one is an even number, can you complete the grid?

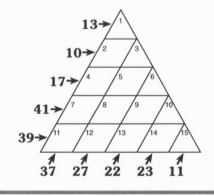

148 FIGURE WORK

Each figure contains a detail that is not present in the other three. Can you spot all four details?

150 DOT-TO-DOT

Join the dots from 1 to 36 to reveal the hidden picture.

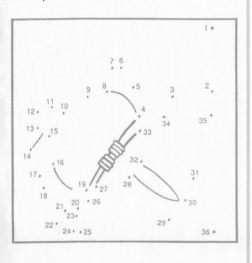

149 RED, WHITE AND BLUE

Each of the squares numbered 1 to 13 is coloured red, white or blue, one colour being represented five times, and the other two colours, four times each. From the clues given below, can you insert the correct colour in each of the squares?

Clues

1 No two adjacent squares vertically or horizontally are the same colour.
2 There is a white square directly to the left of a blue square in the middle horizontal row, which has no other white squares.
3 None of the four isolated squares (numbers 1, 5, 9 and 13) is blue.
4 Two of the four squares denoted by a double-digit number are red.
5 There is just one red square in the horizontal row numbered from 2 to 4.
6 Central square number 7 is red.
7 Squares 1 and 12 are the same colour.
8 One white square has a number which is twice that of a red square.

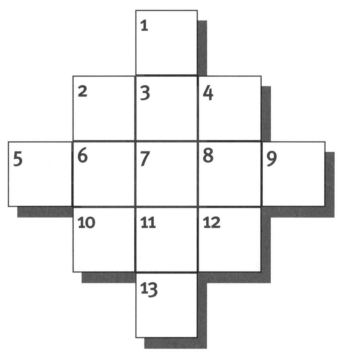

Starting tip: Begin by identifying the blue squares.

151 CUBIT

The square contains the first 16 numbers which are either a square or cube (or both) from 1–169 inclusive. Each row and column contains a one-digit number. When all of the numbers in each row or column are added together, the final digit of the total is shown next to the appropriate row or column. C2 plus A4 equals C3; B4 plus D2 plus one equals A1; C3 has three digits; all in column 1 are odd and all in column 4 are even; A3 is three times C1 and D2 is a multiple of A2.

Can you place each number in the grid?

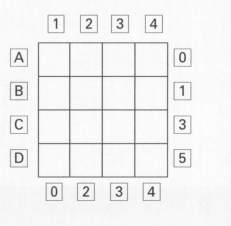

152 WHO'S WHO?

From the information given below can you match each girl to her sister?

153 DROP-OUT

In the top picture, the man is kicking a ball. In the bottom picture, the ball has gone. Which ball did he kick away?

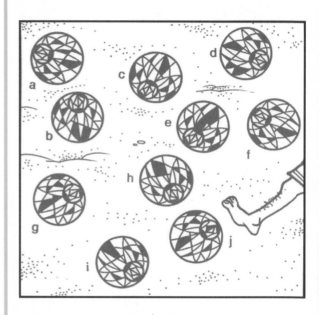

154 CROSSNUMBER

Just like a crossword – but the answer to each clue is a number which is entered by putting one digit into each square. See if you can fill all these empty squares:

ACROSS
1. 7 x 8 – 9
3. 9 x 8 – 7
6. 3 x 3 x 3 x 3
8. 4 x 5 x 6
10. 93 + 99
11. 2 x 2 x 2 x 3
12. 96 / 6
14. 102 – 38
17. 97 – 59
19. 387 – 93
21. 18 x 20
23. 1986 / 3
24. (12 x 8) + 1

DOWN
2. 1000 – 211
4. 29 x 11 – 10
5. 200 / 4
7. 11 x 11
9. 71 + 82 + 93
10. 24 – 8
13. 101 – 38
15. 20 x 20
16. 14 x 14
18. 364 + 475
19. 52 / 2
20. 6 x 7
22. (3 x 9) + (5 x 8)

155 CHRISTMAS PUDDING

The 16 squares in the large square in the diagram each contain one of the letters which make up the phrase CHRISTMAS PUDDING. From the clues given below, can you put the right letter into each of the squares?

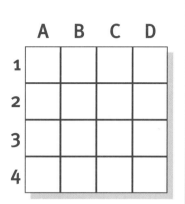

Clues

1 None of the three letters which occur twice in the phrase is in the same vertical, horizontal or diagonal line as its twin.
2 Square A4 contains a letter from the first half of the alphabet.
3 The letter in square D3 is a vowel.
4 The A is immediately to the left of the C, and immediately above one of the Ds.
5 The letter in square B2 is an S, while the T is somewhere in column D.
6 The letter in C3 is not the initial letter of either of the words in the phrase.
7 Both the U and the N are in row 2, the former being further left.
8 The letter in square C4 immediately precedes in the alphabet its neighbour in B4.
9 The letter in square D4 comes earlier in the alphabet than the one in D1.
10 The R can be seen two places to the left of an I.
11 The M and the H appear in the same horizontal row as each other.

Starting tip: Start by placing both of the letters S.

156 SILHOUETTE

Shade in every fragment containing a dot – and what have you got?

157 CODE MASTER

Just follow the rules of that classic puzzle, Master Mind, to crack the colour code. The first number tells you how many of the pegs are exactly correct – the right colour in the right place(✓✓).

The second number tells you how many pegs are the correct colour but are not in the right place(✓). Colours may be repeated in the answer.

By comparing the information given by each line, can you work out which colour goes in which place?

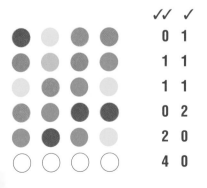

✓✓	✓
0	1
1	1
1	1
0	2
2	0
4	0

158 ISLAND HOPPING

Each circle containing a number represents an island. The object is to connect each island with vertical or horizontal bridges so that:

• The number of bridges is the same as the number inside the island.
• There can be up to two bridges between two islands.
• Bridges cannot cross islands or other bridges.
• There is a continuous path connecting all the islands.

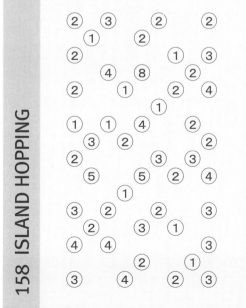

159 SILHOUETTE

Shade in every fragment containing a dot – and what have you got?

160 NUMBER KROSS ●●●

See how quickly you can fit all these numbers into the grid. We've filled one number in to start you off.

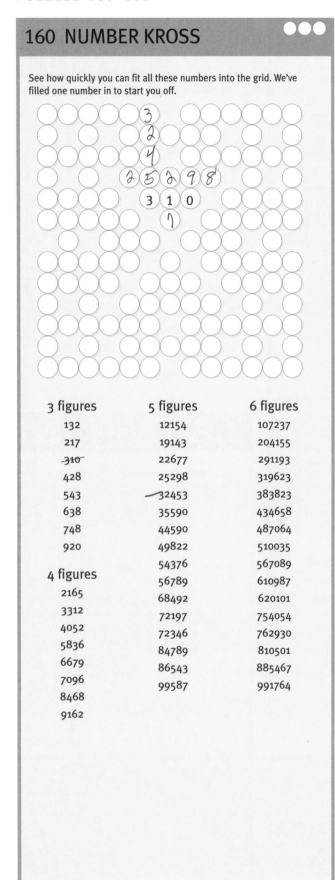

3 figures	5 figures	6 figures
132	12154	107237
217	19143	204155
~~310~~	22677	291193
428	25298	319623
543	~~32453~~	383823
638	35590	434658
748	44590	487064
920	49822	510035
	54376	567089
4 figures	56789	610987
2165	68492	620101
3312	72197	754054
4052	72346	762930
5836	84789	810501
6679	86543	885467
7096	99587	991764
8468		
9162		

161 WHICH CAR?

The game 'Which Car?' is a card game using 36 different cards. Each card depicts a car of a particular make, either a Ford, a Lincoln, or a Chevrolet, a particular model, a sports car, a saloon, or an estate, and the cars are red, green, blue or silver. In this particular game five children took part. They were each dealt seven cards, with the seventh being dealt face up. The 36th card was placed face down on the table. Each player in turn then stated (more or less!) which cards he or she did not have, and then gave an indication of the most or least numbers of cards held of any combination of make, model, or colour. In this game no-one held more than three cards in any category. George's exposed card was a green Ford saloon. He said he had no red and no blue Fords, no Chevrolet sports and no Ford estates.

Anna's exposed card was a green Chevrolet estate. She said she had no Ford sports, no silver Fords, no Ford estates, no red Lincolns and no Chevrolet saloons. Katy's exposed card was a blue Chevrolet saloon. She said she had no red cars, no silver Lincolns and no blue Fords. Richard's exposed card was a silver Lincoln saloon. He said he had no Chevrolet estates, no Lincoln sports, no Ford saloons.

Jane's exposed card was a red Ford sports car. She said she had no red Chevrolet, no Ford saloons, no green Fords, no Chevrolet sports and no silver Lincolns. George then said that he had more blue cars than any other colour and more Lincolns than any other make. He said he had one saloon car, one green car and one silver. Anna said she had more Lincolns than any other make and more saloon cars than any other model, all different colours. She said she had one blue car. Katy said she had more green cars than any other colour and one sports car. She said she had more Chevrolets than any other make, all different models and colours. Richard said he had more Fords than any other make, all different colours. He said he had more estates than any other model, only one green car and more reds than any other colour, plus one silver sports car. Jane said she had more Ford cars than any other make, all different colours, and only one blue car.

At this stage, Richard was able to identify the 36th card because he had failed to declare a further single card of a particular colour. Can you now evaluate each hand and the 36th?

	Ford			Lincoln			Chevrolet		
	Sp	Sa	Es	Sp	Sa	Es	Sp	Sa	Es
Red									
Green									
Blue									
Silver									

162 BREAKTHROUGH ●●

See how quickly you can break this grid down into the 28 dominoes from which it is formed.

6	4	3	1	4	6	5
1	2	1	1	2	0	6
3	6	1	3	5	1	0
6	4	1	3	2	6	0
6	6	5	2	3	0	4
5	0	5	5	3	0	3
0	2	4	3	4	1	2
2	2	4	5	4	5	0

63 BOTTLED UP

Can you help the shop assistant find four identical bottles?

165 IN THE FRAME

There were only four runners in the 3.30 at Shingledown the other day. The diagram shows a head-on view of them lined up for the start. From the clues given below, can you name the horse in each of the starting-stalls lettered A to D, and fully identify its jockey?

Clues

1 As they wait for the off in the starting-stalls Jackie has Mr Jingle immediately on one side of him and the rider named Silk immediately on the other.
2 Derek Raynes is riding a horse somewhere to the left of Placebo as you look at the diagram.
3 Nigel, who is ready for the off in stall C, is not riding Sea Fret.
4 Paddy, whose surname is not Mount, is riding Saturday Night.

Horses: Mr Jingle; Placebo; Saturday Night; Sea Fret
First names: Derek; Jackie; Nigel; Paddy
Surnames: Mount; Raynes; Ryder; Silk

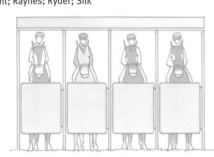

	A	B	C	D
Horse:	_____	_____	_____	_____
First name:	_____	_____	_____	_____
Surname:	_____	_____	_____	_____

Starting tip: First work out which stall Jackie is in.

164 WHO AND HOW FAR?

These facts deal with four men:
1 The carpenter lives due East of Jack.
2 Mr Gainor is older than the dentist.
3 The tallest man lives due North of Len.
4 Mr Fulton lives exactly three miles from the dentist.
5 The artist is taller than Karl.
6 Len is heavier than Mr Fulton.
7 Mr Elton lives exactly two miles from the artist.
8 Jack lives due North of Karl.
9 Mr Gainor is younger than the artist.
10 Mr Fulton is shorter than Karl.
11 Mr Harkness is older than Ike.
12 Mr Fulton lives exactly five miles from the builder.

Exactly how far does the oldest man live from the builder?

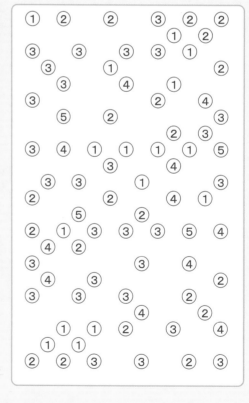

166 ISLAND HOPPING

Each circle containing a number represents an island. The object is to connect each island with vertical or horizontal bridges so that:
• The number of bridges is the same as the number inside the island.
• There can be up to two bridges between two islands.
• Bridges cannot cross islands or other bridges.
• There is a continuous path connecting all the islands.

167 POSER

The artist has made five mistakes while trying to paint an exact portrait of the woman. Can you see what they are?

168 NUMBER KROSS

See how quickly you can fit all these numbers into the grid. We've filled one number in to start you off.

9 5 1 6 7 1
8 7 9 0 0 2 1
2 4 6 7 9 5
9 8 8 4 3 3 2
1 7 0 7 9 2 3
2 0 2 9 1 1
3 2 0 8
4 1 1 8 3 5
2 0 6 7 4 3 5
3 0 3 1 0 6 4
5 2 0 1 2 8 6
5 5 1 9 3 5 3
7 4 6 7 4 0 8

3 figures	5 figures	6 figures
103	10549	160056
208	19353	176802
321	20291	246795
435	32433	263857
530	37064	302960
645	41183	381526
847	47890	410430
923	55213	423557
	56658	504879
4 figures	64755	520128
1707	64980	614809
2067	70310	690560
3214	79287	746740
4134	84332	842710
5670	88017	951671
6786	90021	982912
7998		
8112		

169 ROLL UP

Which one of the seven impressions was made by the roller?

170 SIGHTSEEING

While on holiday in North Africa, four friends went sightseeing round four towns. Can you spot them in all four places?

171 ONBOARD TROUBLE

A dartboard has been divided into eight segments, each with an inner and outer number. The outer numbers are 1–8 and the inner are numbers 9–16. From the following clues, can you determine which number is in each segment? No numbers are the same as the segment number, and none of the outer numbers in a segment are a factor of the inner number of the same segment, except for the number one of course. Twice, the two numbers in a segment add up to 11 and the highest total is 22 which only appears once. The 7 is two places clockwise from the 5 and is diagonally opposite the 2. 1 is on the right-hand side of the board, three places clockwise from the 3. Segment 5 is the only one to contain two even numbers and segment 8, the only one with two odd numbers. The 7 and 16 are in the top half of the board and 15 is in the bottom half. Only one of the inner numbers is twice the segment number. On only one occasion do the two numbers in a segment add up to 19, but never do they total 20.

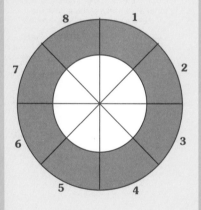

172 TIME OUT

This digital display in Look-No-Hands Watch and Clock Emporium confuses many a passer-by. But if we tell you that one clock is 3 mins out, another is 7 mins out, a third is 14 mins out and the fourth is 20 minutes out you'll soon be able to tell anyone who asks the right time won't you?

173 SET SQUARE

All the digits from 1 to 9 are used in this grid, but only once. Can you work out their positions in the grid and make the sums work? We've given two numbers to start you off.

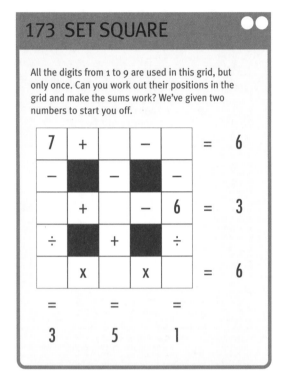

176 ISLAND HOPPING

Each circle containing a number represents an island. The object is to connect each island with vertical or horizontal bridges so that:

• The number of bridges is the same as the number inside the island.
• There can be up to two bridges between two islands.
• Bridges cannot cross islands or other bridges.
• There is a continuous path connecting all the islands.

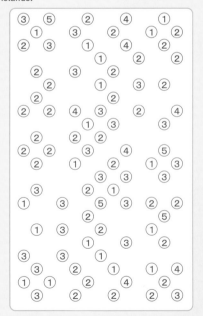

In the five puzzles A, B, C, D and E, can you replace each ? with the right number which fits the pattern?

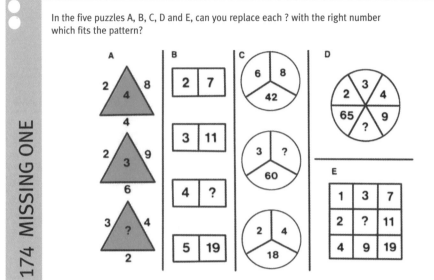

174 MISSING ONE

175 HIT AND MISMATCHES

The letters A–J are entered randomly in the top row so that none is in its correct position, counting left to right, and no two consecutive letters are adjacent. The numbers 2–11 are entered randomly on the bottom row and no two consecutive numbers are adjacent.

The centre row contains pairs of symbols, one plain and one coloured each of type ▭ ▬ ▢ ■ ◯ ⬤ ◯ ● △ ▲ Two coloured symbols occupy the first two squares from the left, and two plain ones are adjacent in the 7th and 8th squares from the left. Elsewhere plain and coloured symbols alternate with no two similar shapes adjacent. A is somewhere left of B and right of G; C is not at either end. I and G are above plain symbols. 6 is below the coloured triangle, and somewhere left of both 9 and the plain rectangle, which are not in the same column. J is above the coloured square which is to the left of both the plain circle and 8 which are not in the same column; 4 is somewhere between 5 to its left, and 11, although not adjacent to either, and is below a coloured symbol. The fourth and fifth letters from the left are vowels; the second and eighth numbers from the left total 14; the coloured circle is three places to the left of the coloured triangle. One column reads H ⬤ 3. F is to the immediate left of B and ⬤ to the immediate left of ▭; 2 is to the immediate left of 6; D is somewhere left of E; ▬ is somewhere to the right of ▢; ◯ is above 7.

Can you match letters, symbols and numbers?

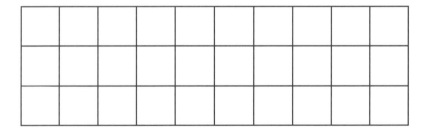

177 LOGISTICAL

Dr Featherbrane, the eminent naturalist and author of The Butterfly in Winter, was the proverbial absent-minded professor. Last week he mislaid his diary, and consequently got his timetable in a complete muddle. Can you sort out which vital item was missing on each day, which appointment he should have kept each day and which one he mistakenly went to on each day?

Clues

A Thursday was the actual day of the awards ceremony, but not the day the professor turned up, minus his notes, to give a lecture to an empty hall. The latter occasion occurred later in the week than the day he mistakenly set off for the awards ceremony.

B Professor Featherbrane spent Wednesday afternoon searching for his missing spectacles whilst waiting in vain for his students to turn up for tutorials. The interview board did not feature in any way on either this day or Friday, when he left his briefcase at home.

C On the day the professor should have gone to the faculty meeting, he travelled up to New York for an awards ceremony. Not an easy operation, as this was the day he had left his wallet behind!

Record in this grid all the information obtained from the clues, by using a cross to indicate a definite 'no' and a tick to show a definite 'yes'. Transfer these to all sections of the grid thus eliminating all but one possibility, which must be the correct one.

Day	Missing item	Appointment	Error

178 NETWORK TV

Can you spot the eight differences between these two pictures?

179 FILLING IN

Each of the letters in the boxes contains a different digit from 1 to 9. As is our usual practice, each calculation is to be treated sequentially rather than according to the 'multiplication first' system. Can you fill in the empty boxes?

	+		−		= 5
+		x		−	
	x		−		= 3
÷		−		x	
	x		÷		= 2
= 3		= 8		= 9	

180 MONSTER MATCH

Which two of these monsters are exactly the same?

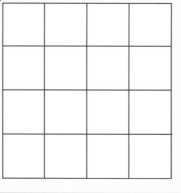

181 SQUARE NUMBERS

The numbers 1–25 are arranged randomly so that no two consecutive numbers are adjacent in any direction. One number has been entered for you. The four corner numbers are all multiples of three and no other multiples of three are adjacent to them or to each other. The long diagonal from top left to bottom right totals 72 and the other from top right to bottom left totals 61, each diagonal containing two consecutive numbers. In column 1 the lowest number is 8; 25 is somewhere in column 2; in row E the highest number is 17. The number in B2 is twice D2 and half of E2. The number in D4 is four higher than that in D1, and equals B4 plus D3, the latter being half B5. C1 is five higher than D1; A3 plus A4 totals 23; and 24 is a chess knight's move from the 25. 10 is further left than 11 although they are in the same row; 13 and 19 are in the row below.

Can you locate each number?

	1	2	3	4	5
A					
B					
C				3	
D					
E					

183 SQUARED OFF

This empty 4 x 4 grid was originally filled with the numbers from 1 to 16 inclusive. No two consecutive numbers were adjacent (including diagonally) or in the same row or column. Each of the sixteen numbers given in the full grid is the sum of the horizontal and vertical neighbours of the corresponding square in the original grid. Can you work out where the sixteen numbers originally were?

20	21	24	17
23	41	40	25
39	28	40	28
5	37	14	19

182 ISLAND HOPPING

Each circle containing a number represents an island. The object is to connect each island with vertical or horizontal bridges so that:
• The number of bridges is the same as the number inside the island.
• There can be up to two bridges between two islands.
• Bridges cannot cross islands or other bridges.
• There is a continuous path connecting all the islands.

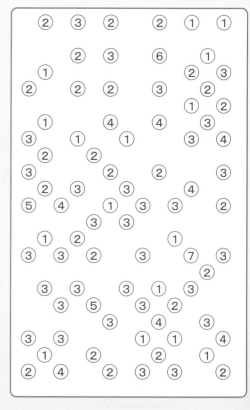

184 FILLING IN

Each of the nine empty boxes contains a digit from 1 to 9. The same digit can be used several times. As is our usual practice, each calculation is to be treated sequentially rather than according to the 'multiplication first' system. Can you fill in the empty boxes so that the calculations are correct both vertically and horizontally?

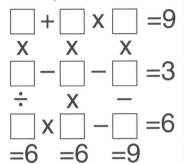

185 CELL STRUCTURE

The object is to create white areas surrounded by black walls, so that:
• Each white area contains only one number.
• The number of cells in a white area is equal to the number in it.
• The white areas are separated from each other with a black wall.
• Cells containing numbers must not be filled in.
• The black cells must be linked into a continuous wall.
• Black cells cannot form a square of 2 x 2 or larger.

3			4	3			
	2						
							2
4				2		4	
			3				
2				1			
		2					
			4		4		2

186 FIGURE IT OUT

Each figure from 1–9 appears four times in the square, no two similar digits being diagonally adjacent; where the same digit appears more than once in any row or column, this is stated. Can you complete the square?

Row

1 Two 4s and two 9s alternating; total 34
2 One even, two odd, two even, one odd digit, from left to right; lowest is 2; total 37
3 Two 1s separated by an 8; two 5s but no 4s
4 Two adjacent 6s with an odd digit and two 8s
5 Two 3s separated by a 6; highest is a 7; total 22
6 Two adjacent 7s; total 24

Column

1 Two 8s separated by an odd digit; total 29
2 Two adjacent 9s; the other digits also total 18
3 Two adjacent 2s; total 27
4 Two 9s separated by two digits; total 31
5 Two 6s separated by two digits, all bracketed by two odd digits
6 Total 22

	1	2	3	4	5	6
1						
2						
3						
4						
5						
6						

187 SNAIL TRAIL

Can you find a path through the maze, starting from the snail's nose and finishing in the bottom right-hand corner.

59

188 MAZE MYSTERY

Travel from the entrance to the exit of the maze, filling the path completely to create a picture.

189 CARDS ON THE TABLE

The 13 cards of a suit are shuffled and dealt out in a row, and it is found that none is in its correct numerical position (Ace left, King right), and the court cards are not at either end or adjacent to each other. The Ace is between 9 (left) and 8, 4 between Queen (left) and Jack, 2 two places left of 10, 7 two places left of 3, the left-hand card one higher than the right-hand card, and the King is left of the Queen. The 9th and 10th cards from the left total 9, the 9th being of lower value. Can you locate each card?

191 FIGURE IT OUT

The digits 1–9 each appear four times in the grid, and no two squares which are adjacent horizontally or vertically contain the same digit. Every instance of a digit's occurring more than once in a row or column is mentioned in the clues.

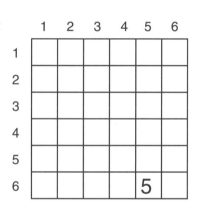

Across
1 A pair of 3s; the last three digits reversed are one-third of the first three digits
2 A pair of 1s but no 4s; the total is 19
3 A pair of 2s enclosing an 8; the total is 30
4 A pair of 4s; the total is 35
5 A pair of 8s but no 6s; the total is 41
6 8 is the highest number and 1 the lowest; the total is 31

Down
1 A pair of 9s; the total is 42
2 A pair of 6s enclosing a 3; there are no 8s
3 A pair of 4s; the total is 19
4 A pair of 1s; the total is 28
5 A pair of 2s but no 4s; the total is 25
6 A pair of 9s but no 1s; the total is 35

190 NUMBER KROSS

See how quickly you can fit all these numbers into the grid. We've filled one number in to start you off.

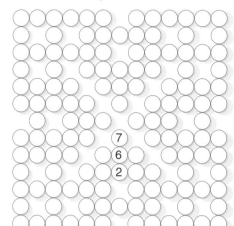

3 figures	5 figures	6 figures
184	10179	123579
287	20507	166266
395	22458	220179
499	30254	223344
571	31007	345678
672	47555	357913
~~762~~	47742	441133
863	50923	443322
	51206	556677
4 figures	62918	566333
1918	63459	601714
2016	78957	678135
3172	81633	721233
4958	84156	765432
5661	92107	803917
6294	97980	912005
7676		
9737		

192 A BARGIN TO BOOT

The diagram shows four neighbouring stalls at a car boot sale each selling an assortment of bric-a-brac. From the clues given below, can you identify the person in charge of each of the stalls lettered A to D and say which customer was buying which item from which stall at the particular moment in question?

Clues
1 Lesley bought something from Ken, whose stall was separated by just one other from the one where the fire irons were offered for sale.
2 The vase was sold at stall B.
3 Norman, who did not buy the paperback books, was the customer at stall C, which was not run by Ted.
4 Elsie's stall is lettered A in the diagram; her customer was not Ray.

Stall-holders: Elsie; Ken; Mary; Ted
Customers: Lesley; Norman; Penny; Ray
Item bought: books; fire irons; radio; vase

Starting tip: Begin by working out which stall sold the fire irons.

Customers:
Purchase:

193 MONKEY PUZZLE

In a negative, everything which is really black appears white and everything which is really white appears black. Can you tell which one of the six monkeys is shown as a negative in the top left-hand corner?

194 CUT THE DEAL

Four people about to play cards cut for deal. The cards, which were all of different suits, are shown in the diagram, numbered 1 to 4 in the order in which they were cut. From the clues given below, can you work out the denomination and suit of each card, and name the player who drew it?

Clues
1 Clara made her cut immediately before the King was drawn.
2 The Diamond was cut next but one after the 3, a male player making the intervening cut.
3 Betty's card, which was not a Club, was a lower one than card 4.
4 Adam, whose card was a Heart, drew it some time before the 10 was cut.
5 The second card to be drawn was a black one.

Denominations: 3; 7; 10; King
Suits: Clubs; Diamonds; Hearts; Spades
Players: Adam; Betty; Clara; Dave

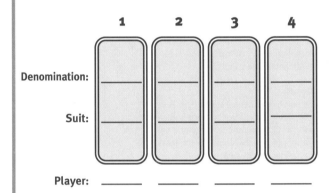

Denomination:

Suit:

Player:

Starting tip: Begin by working out who cut card 4.

195 SYMBOLIC

Can you see which two small rectangles contain the same four symbols?

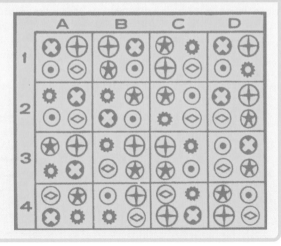

196 BLACK OUT

Which one of these letters was printed with the reverse stamp shown at the top?

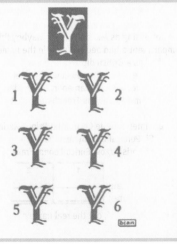

197 SPOT THE DIFFERENCE

See how quickly you can spot the ten differences between these two clowns.

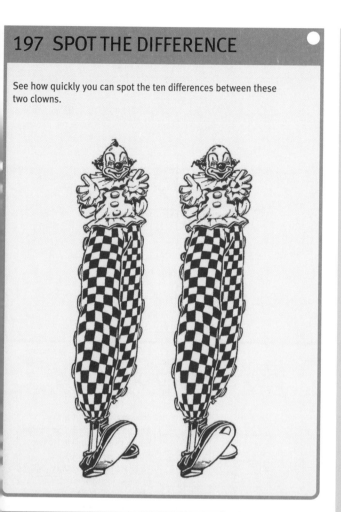

There are eight differences between the two cartoons. Can you spot them?

198 THAT LITTLE BIT OF DIFFERENCE

199 ORIENT EXPRESS ALIASES

One day in the late 1920s, the *chef de train* of the Orient Express received a discreet warning that the passengers in the first four sleeping compartments were – well, not all they appeared to be. From the clues given below, can you work out the name in which each compartment had been reserved, and uncover the real name of its occupant?

Clues

1 Maxwell Van Skyler, the notorious American confidence trickster, occupied the compartment next to that of the man masquerading as Danish physicst professor Nils Knudsen.
2 The man in compartment 4, who was not Russian spy Boris Zugov, was not posing as Middle Eastern playboy Prince Karim Al-Aziz.
3 Compartment 2 had been booked in the name of Sir Percival Gascoyne, described as a British diplomat.
4 Enrico Leone, the Italian jewel thief, travelled in compartment 1.
5 Franz Schmidt, the German anarchist, had the next compartment but one to the man posing as French aristocrat the Duc de Chomette.

Assumed names: Duc de Chomette; Prince Karim Al-Aziz; Professor Nils Knudsen; Sir Percival Gascoyne.
Real names; Boris Zugov; Enrico Leone; Franz Schmidt; Maxwell Van Skyler

	1	2	3	4
Alias:	___	___	___	___
Real name:	___	___	___	___

Starting tip: First work out the real name of the passenger in compartment 4.

200 PLUGGED IN

Which one of the four leads should the guitarist plug into the loudspeaker?

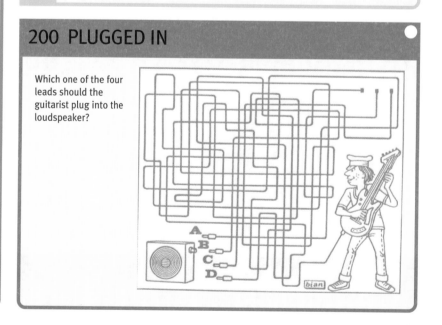

201 CIRCLE ROUND

The diagram shows four straight lines whose extremities are numbered I to VIII. Each of the arms numbered I to VIII has two circles, in the inner of which appears a different one of the numerals 1 to 8 and in the outer of which is contained a different one of the letters A to H. From the clues given below can you fill in correctly all the numbers and letters?

Clues

1 The word HAG may be read anti-clockwise on the outer ring; all of its letters are accompanied by even digits on the inner ring.

2 The 8 and the 7 are on the same straight line which bears even Roman numerals at each end, the 8 end having a higher numeral than the 7 end.

3 The letter at position III is the B.

4 The numeral on arm V and the one on the arm directly opposite the one bearing the A total the number on arm IV.

5 The 5 is on the arm numbered I in the diagram.

6 The letter in position VI is a vowel.

7 The 1, which is not on the same straight line as the 6, is on an arm numbered two higher than the one occupied by the C.

8 The letter on arm IV has an earlier position in the alphabet than the one on arm II, but does not come immediately before it.

Letters: A; B; C; D; E; F; G; H
Numerals: 1; 2; 3; 4; 5; 6; 7; 8

Starting tip: Begin by positioning the H.

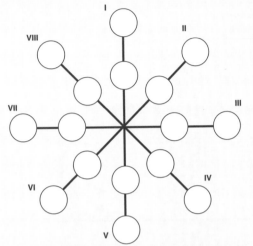

202 CELL STRUCTURE

The object is to create white areas surrounded by black walls, so that:
* Each white area contains only one number
* The number of cells in a white area is equal to the number in it
* The white areas are separated from each other with a black wall
* Cells containing numbers must not be filled in
* The black cells must be linked into a continuous wall
* Black cells cannot form a square of 2 x 2 or larger

203 SQUARED OFF

The empty 4 x 4 grid was originally filled with the numbers from 1 to 16 inclusive. No two consecutive numbers were adjacent (including diagonally) or in the same row or column. Each of the sixteen numbers given in the full grid is the sum of the horizontal and vertical neighbours of the corresponding square in the original grid. Can you work out where the sixteen numbers originally were?

20	23	15	25
17	37	37	20
42	23	41	21
11	41	13	24

204 DARTING ABOUT

A dart player scores 85 with three darts hitting a treble, a double and a single (no bulls). Given that the three numbers that he hits add up to 43 and that the difference between the largest and smallest numbers is 6, can you work out how his score is made up?

Treble   Double   Single

205 SILHOUETTE

Shade in every fragment containing a dot – and what have you got?

206 IT'S MAGIC

This magic square can be completed using every other number from 23 to 71. To give you a start, we have entered every digit 3 and all the numbers which are multiples of 3. Can you complete the square so that the five numbers in each row, column and diagonal add up to the magic total? That total – and close your eyes now if you don't want to be told – is 235.

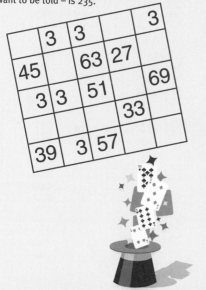

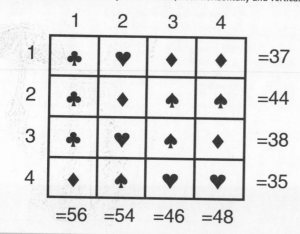

207 EURO SQUARE

Each of the sixteen small squares in the diagram contains one of the numbers 1 to 4 in words, in either English, French, German or Italian, as listed below. From the clues given below, can you write the correct word in each square?

Clues

1 Each of columns A, B, C and D contains one number in each of the four different languages.

2 Quatre is the number in square B2.

3 The number in B1 is twice that in D2, both being in the same language.

4 Two is in the horizontal row above the one containing both zwei and due.

5 The even number in D3 is not in French.

6 Tre is immediately to the right of four, and immediately above vier.

7 Quattro is somewhere in column D.

8 The German number in column C is drei; but its right-hand neighbour is not in German; D1 does not contain eins.

9 The number in A4 is one higher than the one in A1, though, of course, the language is different.

10 The numbers in D1 and C3 are in the same language, the former being the higher of the two.

English: one; two; three; four
French: un; deux; trois; quatre
German: eins; zwei; drei; vier
Italian: uno; due; tre; quattro

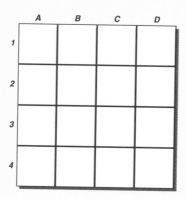

Starting tip: Begin by identifying the number in B1.

208 SYMBOLISM

Each of the four symbols (Heart, Club, Diamond and Spade) represents a certain number in all the rows across – and the totals refer to the sum of the symbols shown on that row using these numbers.

Each symbol also refers to a number (it may or may not be the same number as that in the rows across!) when used in the sums downwards, with totals at the bottom of the grid – the symbols in each column add up to the totals at the bottom; and each symbol is the same number for all the downwards sums.

Can you work out the value of the symbols shown, both horizontally and vertically?

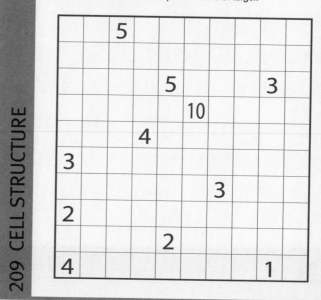

209 CELL STRUCTURE

The object is to create white areas surrounded by black walls, so that:
* Each white area contains only one number.
* The number of cells in a white area is equal to the number in it.
* The white areas are separated from each other with a black wall.
* Cells containing numbers must not be filled in.
* The black cells must be linked into a continuous wall.
* Black cells cannot form a square of 2 x 2 or larger.

210 DOT-TO-DOT

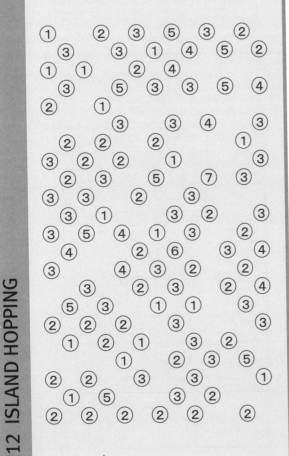

Join the dots from 1 to 37 to reveal the hidden picture.

211 GHOST STOREYS

Ghastleigh Castle has four towers, and each tower has a haunted room. From the clues below, can you fill in on the plan the name of each tower and its haunted room, and identify the ghost that manifests itself there?

Clues

1 The so-called King's Chamber (Charles II spent a night there while hiding from The Roundheads) is in tower C.

2 The Sorcerer's Den is, unsurprisingly, in the Sorcerer's Tower, which is the next in alphabetical order after the New Tower (built in 1340) where Lady Edith's ghost haunts the scene of her murder.

3 The Whistling Room – the sound comes from the badly-built chimney, not the resident phantom – isn't in Drogo's Tower, named after the original builder of the castle.

4 Brother Luke appears in the tower marked A on the plan; Tower B isn't haunted by Lord Ivo, and isn't the location of the Treasure Room, where the Ghastleigh family silver is still stored.

Tower Names: Black Tower; Drogo's Tower; New Tower; Sorcerer's Tower
Room Names: King's Chamber; Sorcerer's Den; Treasure Room; Whistling Room
Ghosts: Brother Luke; Lady Edith; Lord Ivo; Old Meg

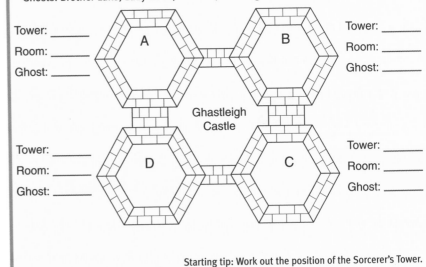

Tower: _____
Room: _____
Ghost: _____

Tower: _____
Room: _____
Ghost: _____

Tower: _____
Room: _____
Ghost: _____

Tower: _____
Room: _____
Ghost: _____

Starting tip: Work out the position of the Sorcerer's Tower.

212 ISLAND HOPPING

Each circle containing a number represents an island. The object is to connect each island with vertical or horizontal bridges so that:

* The number of bridges is the same as the number inside the island.
* There can be up to two bridges between two islands.
* Bridges cannot cross islands or other bridges.
* There is a continuous path connecting all the islands.

① ② ③ ⑤ ③ ②
③ ③ ① ④ ⑤ ②
① ① ② ④
③ ⑤ ③ ③ ⑤ ④
② ①
③ ③ ④ ③
② ③ ② ①
③ ② ② ① ③
② ③ ⑤ ⑦ ③
③ ③ ② ③
③ ① ③ ② ③
③ ⑤ ④ ① ③ ②
④ ② ⑥ ③ ④
③ ④ ③ ② ②
③ ② ③ ② ④
⑤ ③ ① ① ③
② ② ② ③ ③
① ② ① ③ ②
① ② ③ ⑤
② ② ③ ③ ①
① ⑤ ③ ②
② ② ② ② ② ②

213 FILLING IN

Each of the letters in the boxes contains a different digit from 1 to 9. As is our usual practice, each calculation is to be treated sequentially rather than according to the 'multiplication first' system. Can you fill in the empty boxes?

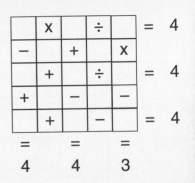

	X	÷		= 4
−		+	X	
	+	÷		= 4
+		−	−	
	+		−	= 4
= 4	= 4	= 3		

214 SKELETON SUMS

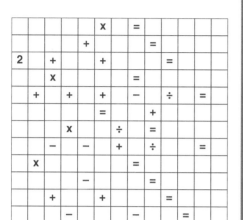

Insert the following numbers into the spaces on each horizontal line so as to form thirteen valid equations, treating each calculation sequentially rather than according to the 'multiplication first' system. When the numbers are correctly placed, the digits in each vertical column will total 45.

2 2 3 4 5 5 6 7 7 7 8 9 9 9

14 18 18 19 24 25 30 36 39 42 45 90 96

168 200 249 397 439 439 566 574 622 675 700

1089 1425 1711 2323 2587 2889 9991

10009 11545 36218 42546 69270 85092

215 BY THE SEASIDE

The diagram shows four children paddling in the sea, while their respective mothers sit in deck-chairs on the beach keeping a watchful eye on them. From the clues given below, can you identify the four children lettered A to D and the four mothers numbered 1 to 4, and match them up correctly?

Clues

1 None of the children is indicated by a letter whose position in the alphabet is equivalent to the number denoting his or her mother.
2 As they sit facing out to sea Jill is immediately to the right of Emma's mum, and immediately to the left of the mother of child D.
3 Jack is the son of Francesca, who is not in deck-chair 3.
4 Karen is paddling two positions to the left (facing the sea) of Lesley's child.

Children: Damien; Emma; Jack; Karen
Mothers: Francesca; Jill; Lesley; Sally

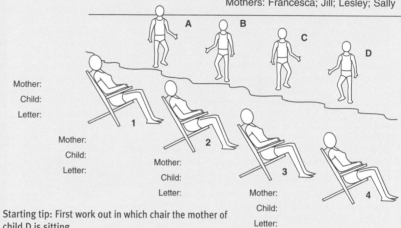

Starting tip: First work out in which chair the mother of child D is sitting.

217 SQUARED OFF

The (almost) empty 4 x 4 grid was originally filled with the numbers from 1 to 16 inclusive. No two consecutive numbers were adjacent horizontally, vertically or diagonally. Each of the sixteen numbers given in the full grid is the sum of the horizontal and vertical neighbours of the corresponding square in the original grid. Given the starter 1, can you work out where the sixteen numbers originally were?

		1	

28	21	27	8
18	35	30	25
33	28	25	31
6	25	32	18

216 CARDS ON THE TABLE

The 13 cards of a suit are shuffled and dealt in a line. None is in its correct position counting from the Ace left to right, no court cards are at either end, but two of the court cards are adjacent, with the other three places to the right. 4 is two places left of 9, 5 two places left of 8, 10 two places left of 6, 7 two left of the Ace, the King three left of 2, the Queen two left of 3, and the Jack three right of the Ace. The centre card is not a court card. Where the Jack equals 11, the Queen equals 12, the King equals 13, the two end cards total 13 and the 3rd and 4th total 10.
Can you locate each card?

218 KRIS KROSS

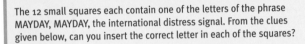

Fit the numbers into the grid. To get you started, one has been done for you.

2 figures
~~955~~
10
21
33
42
54
56
79
87
88
95

3 figures
170
186
222
260
306
402
519
548
663
791
884
889
917

4 figures
1276
2245
3093
5386
6482
7910
8218
9977

5 figures
16650
20476
68308
90759

6 figures
154564
338085
416707
720503
896952
919350

7 figures
1469353
3857292
4629390
4959018
5267489
6357655

9 figures
624114298
967753780

11 figures
36870152598
41479036525
70264293061
96762458813

219 ISLANDS IN THE SUN

Four couples booked holidays on different islands for themselves and their two children. From the clues given below, can you match the couples, work out their surnames and the names of their children, and say which island paradise each foursome visited?

Clues

1 Rebecca is Charles' sister.

2 Keith and Angela's son is not the boy named Darren Morris.

3 Judy Langton's holiday location was not Cyprus, and her son's name is not Ian.

4 Chris is Garry's father, and Gail is the daughter of Lance, who did not visit the Canaries.

5 Violet is Fiona's mother; she is not married to Perry, and she is not Mrs Chadwick, who spent her holiday in Crete.

6 Bridget and her husband took their children to Majorca.

Husband	Wife	Surname	Son	Daughter	Location

220 A CRY FOR HELP

The 12 small squares each contain one of the letters of the phrase MAYDAY, MAYDAY, the international distress signal. From the clues given below, can you insert the correct letter in each of the squares?

Clues

1 No identical letter appears in adjacent squares vertically or horizontally.

2 The combination A above D can be seen in one vertical column.

3 Letter Y occurs once only in column 2.

4 The letter M is to be inserted in square B2.

5 No D appears in horizontal row D.

6 All four letters in column 1 are different.

7 The different letters in B3 and D3 are not repeated elsewhere in that column.

Letters check-list: A; A; A; A; D; D; M; M; Y; Y; Y; Y

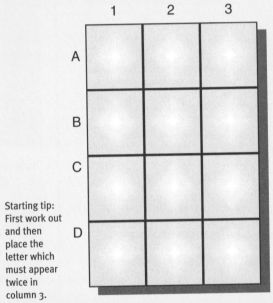

Starting tip:
First work out and then place the letter which must appear twice in column 3.

221 CELL STRUCTURE

The object is to create white areas surrounded by black walls, so that:
* Each white area contains only one number
* The number of cells in a white area is equal to the number in it
* The white areas are separated from each other with a black wall
* Cells containing numbers must not be filled in
* The black cells must be linked into a continuous wall
* Black cells cannot form a square of 2 x 2 or larger

222 IT FIGURES

Place a number from 1 to 9 in each empty cell so that the sum of each vertical or horizontal block equals the number at the top or on the left of that block. Numbers may only be used once in each block.

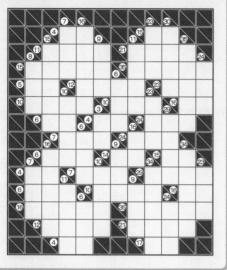

225 SUM WAY DOWN

In the top line, the circles, A to E, are to be filled with two digits each, using between them, each digit (0,1,2,3,4,5,6,7,8,9) just once only; so 0,1,3,8 need placing. From then on, the number in each circle is the sum of the digits in the two circles which are above it and joined to it by a line. Thus circle H will contain the answer to 5+2+6+7. When filled in correctly, the circles will contain fifteen different numbers.

Given those already in position, can you complete the picture?

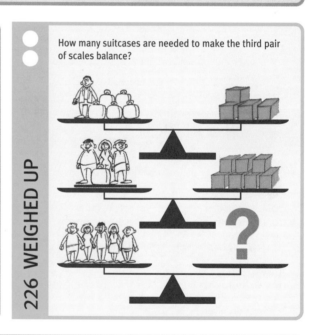

223 CELL STRUCTURE

The object is to create white areas surrounded by black walls, so that:
* Each white area contains only one number.
* The number of cells in a white area is equal to the number in it.
* The white areas are separated from each other with a black wall.
* Cells containing numbers must not be filled in.
* The black cells must be linked into a continuous wall.
* Black cells cannot form a square of 2 x 2 or larger.

3	2		3		
				3	
2		2			
4		5	1		
5					
		5		3	
2		5			
3	1		1		
				3	
2	3	2			
2					
4		3			
2	2	4			

224 PAIRED UP

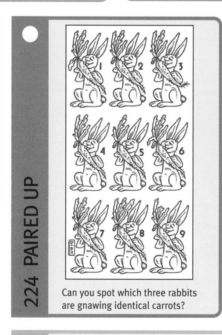

Can you spot which three rabbits are gnawing identical carrots?

226 WEIGHED UP

How many suitcases are needed to make the third pair of scales balance?

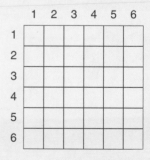

227 FIGURE IT OUT

The digits 1–9 each appear four times in the grid, and no two squares which are adjacent horizontally or vertically contain the same digit. Each instance of a digit occurring more than once in a row or column is mentioned in the clues.

ACROSS
1 A pair of 6s; but no 9; the sum is 36
2 A pair of 1s; 7 is the second highest number; the sum is 23
3 A pair of 5s; but no 7s; the sum is 34
4 A pair of 2s, but no 7s; the sum is 28
5 A pair of 8s; the sum is 36
6 A pair of 1s; 9 is the highest number

DOWN
1 A pair of 6s; the sum is 41
2 A pair of 5s enclosing a 1
3 A pair of 7s; the sum is 35
4 A pair of 6s and a pair of 4s; the sum is 25
5 A pair of 9s; the sum is 39
6 A pair of 1s; the sum is 16

	1	2	3	4	5	6
1						
2						
3						
4						
5						
6						

228 PILE UP

These piles of bricks aren't the random results of a child's play but clues to a final, at present blank, pile on the right. Like the rest, that one has six bricks each with a different one of the six letters. The numbers below the heaps tell you two things:

(a) The number of adjacent pairs of bricks in that column which also appear adjacent in the final pile.

(b) The number of adjacent pairs of bricks that make a correct pair but the wrong way up.

So:

would score one in the 'Correct' row if the final heap had an A directly above a C and a one in the 'Reversed' row if the final heap had a C on top of an A. From all this, can you create the final pile before it topples?

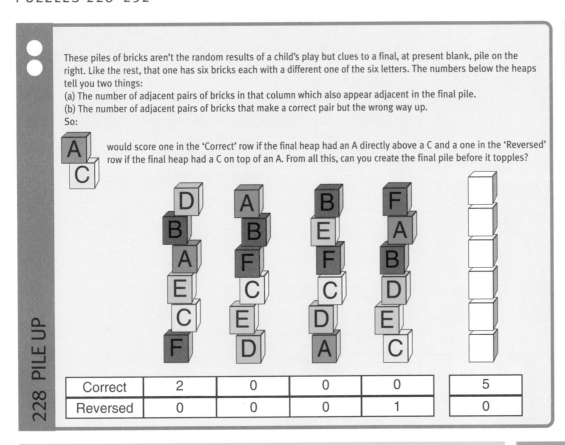

Correct	2	0	0	0	5
Reversed	0	0	0	1	0

229 CAN YOU DIGIT?

ACROSS
1 Add 1 to the square of (6 across + 7 across + 2 down + 11 down)
6 Subtract (4 down plus 1) from 7 across
7 Multiply 2 down's second digit by 19
8 Cube (11 down minus 1)
9 First two digits of 8 across
11 Add 3 to the square of 4 down's first digit
12 Square (11 across + 2 down)

DOWN
1 Square (7 across + 4 down + 10 down)
2 Reverse (7 across reversed minus 1)
3 Cube 11 down
4 Reverse (7 across plus 1)
5 Square (7 across + 11 across + 10 down +11 down)
10 Third and fourth digits of 3 down
11 Subtract 2 from 11 across

1	2	3	4	5
6			7	
8				
9	10		11	
12				

230 DARTING ABOUT

A dart player scores 85 with three darts hitting a treble, a double and a single (no bulls). Given that the three numbers he hits add up to 40 and that the difference between the largest and smallest numbers is 6, can you work out how his score is made up?

Treble   Double   Single

231 SQUARED OFF

The empty 4 x 4 grid was originally filled with the numbers from 1 to 16 inclusive. No two consecutive numbers were adjacent (including diagonally) or in the same row or column. Each of the sixteen numbers given in the full grid is the sum of the horizontal and vertical neighbours of the corresponding square in the original grid. Can you work out where the sixteen numbers originally were?

8	28	20	12
36	22	32	28
9	48	38	27
28	17	35	24

232 BACKHANDER

Which one of these five archers is seen from the back in the top left-hand corner?

233 LENGTH IS STRENGTH

Four bridge players, seated in the traditional positions North, South, East and West (the two former being partners against the two latter), each picked up a hand with a different long suit, but a different length in each case. From the clues given below, can you name the player in each seat, match him with his long suit, and say how many cards of that suit he held?

Clues

1 Ruff had more of his suit than his partner had in Clubs, which was his long suit.

2 Trumpet had a suit longer than that of the player who held the long Diamonds.

3 South's long suit had only five cards in it.

4 East's suit was Hearts.

5 Pass was the player in the North seat.

6 It was Bidding's partner at the table who had the longest suit of all.

Names: Bidding; Pass; Ruff; Trumpet
Suits: Clubs; Diamonds; Hearts; Spades
Length: 5; 6; 7; 8

Starting tip: Begin by working out Ruff's seat.

Name: _____
Suit: _____
Length: _____

```
        N
  W         E
        S
```

Name: _____
Suit: _____
Length: _____

Name: _____
Suit: _____
Length: _____

Name: _____
Suit: _____
Length: _____

234 SNAPPY

Which one of the six photographs of the model was taken as she posed below?

235 FLOOR SHOW

The diagram shows the floor plan of the first floor of a family house, on which are the bedrooms of four children. Each room has recently been re-carpeted in a different colour. From the clues given below, can you name the occupant of each of the rooms numbered 1 to 4, work out his or her age, and identify the colour of the new carpet?

Clues

1 Gemma's new blue carpet is in one of the front bedrooms.

2 James, who is 13, has a room numbered two lower on the plan than the one in which the green carpet has just been laid, whose occupant is 11.

3 The oldest of the four children, who is not Liam, has bedroom number 3.

4 Colette's room does not have the brown carpet.

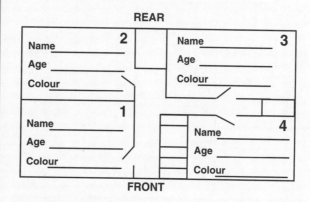

REAR

	2			3
Name			Name	
Age			Age	
Colour			Colour	

	1			4
Name			Name	
Age			Age	
Colour			Colour	

FRONT

Names: Colette; Gemma; James; Liam
Ages: 11; 13; 15; 17
Colours: blue; brown; green; grey

Starting tip: Start by working out the number of the youngest child's room.

236 MAZE MYSTERY

Travel from the entrance to the exit of the maze, filling the path completely to create a picture.

Place a number from 1 to 9 in each empty cell so that the sum of each vertical or horizontal block equals the number at the top or on the left of that block. Numbers may only be used once in each block.

237 IT FIGURES

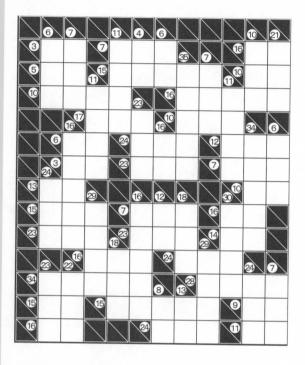

239 LOTTERY, EXTRA, EXTRA

Here's a chance to get your own back on those unkind lottery numbers – at least you can cross a lot of them out and score points! Start by choosing a number and circling it, then cross out every other number that divides exactly into it. If, say, your first choice were 12, you would have to cross out 1, 2, 3, 4 and 6 as they all go into 12 exactly. There is only one rule governing your choice of number – it must be such that at least one other number, which has not been crossed out before, is now crossed out. The game ends when you cannot circle any further numbers.

Your points total is the sum of all the numbers you have circled.

What is the greatest possible score?

1	2	3	4	5	6	7
8	9	10	11	12	13	14
15	16	17	18	19	20	21
22	23	24	25	26	27	28
29	30	31	32	33	34	35
36	37	38	39	40	41	42
43	44	45	46	47	48	49

238 CELL STRUCTURE

The object is to create white areas surrounded by black walls, so that:
* Each white area contains only one number.
* The number of cells in a white area isequal to the number in it.
* The white areas are separated from each other with a black wall.
* Cells containing numbers must not be filled in.
* The black cells must be linked into a continuous wall.
* Black cells cannot form a square of 2 x 2 or larger.

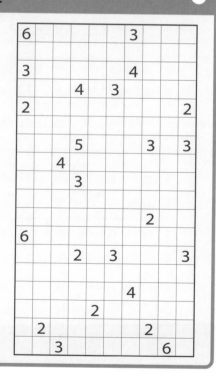

240 NUMBER HEX

What number belongs in the hexagon marked '?'?

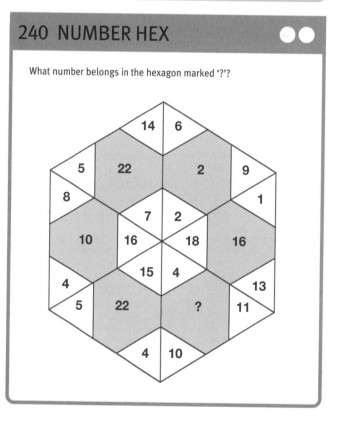

241 IDENTICAL TWINS

Mr Fix-it is doing some work in his garden. Can you spot the two numbered pictures which are identical?

242 BOX CLEVER

Which one of the numbered boxes will be formed when the pattern is folded up correctly?

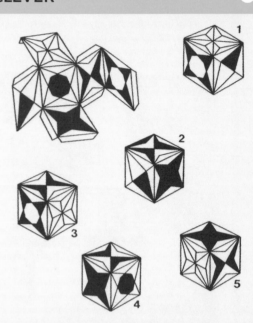

243 LOGISTICAL

Five novels make up Letitia Perowne's Malthouse Saga, which tells the story of a landowning New England family from 1780 to 1977. From the clues below, can you work out the period covered by each title, and the forenames of the family members who are the book's main male and female characters?

Clues

1 *Chronicle*, which deals with the life and adventures of Vaughan Malthouse and his headstrong wife, is not the novel covering the period 1938–1977 which features Claudia Malthouse as its heroine.

2 Joseph and Miriam appear first as childhood sweethearts, then lovers, and finally husband and wife.

3 *Birthright*, which begins on the eve of the First World War, doesn't tell the story of Eugenie's rebellion against her overbearing husband.

4 Major Lambert Malthouse isn't the hero of *Testament*.

5 *Heritage*, the volume of the saga which features the tragic story of Rosalind Malthouse and her faithless husband, neither begins nor ends in 1830, the year of Samuel's birth.

6 Hannah Malthouse features in a volume two earlier in the series than the one which details the life and mysterious death of Esmond.

	1780–1830	1830–1881	1881–1914	1914–1938	1938–1977	Esmond	Joseph	Lambert	Samuel	Vaughan	Claudia	Eugenie	Hannah	Miriam	Rosalind
Birthright															
Chronicle															
Domain															
Heritage															
Testament															
Claudia															
Eugenie															
Hannah															
Miriam															
Rosalind															
Esmond															
Joseph															
Lambert															
Samuel															
Vaughan															

Record in this grid all the information obtained from the clues, by using a cross to indicate a definite 'no' and a tick to show a definite 'yes'. Transfer these to all sections of the grid thus eliminating all but one possibility, which must be the correct one.

Title	Period	Male character	Female character

244 DAILY DOZEN

Here's a gentle mental exercise. Each of the 12 squares contains a different one of the numbers 1 to 12. From the clues given below, can you place them correctly?

Clues

1 The 12 is in square B2; the numbers immediately to its left and diagonally below it to the left are both factors of it, one being an odd number (although not 1).

2 The 6 is adjacent to the 10 in the same row, and is to be found in the same vertical column as the 8.

3 The numbers in squares A1 and C3, added together, give the one in square C4.

4 The 7 is immediately below the 4, and immediately to the right of the 5.

5 Neither the 2 nor the 1 is in column 1, though the 2 is in a column further left than the one containing the 11.

Numbers: 1; 2; 3; 4; 5; 6; 7; 8; 9; 10; 11; 12

Starting tip: First place the numbers referred to in clue 1.

	1	2	3	4
A				
B				
C				

NB The numbers which are factors of 12 are 1, 2, 3, 4 and 6.

245 IT FIGURES

Place a number from 1 to 9 in each empty cell so that the sum of each vertical or horizontal block equals the number at the top or on the left of that block. Numbers may only be used once in each block.

246 SHADOWS

There's nothing a dragon likes better than a mug of cocoa to round off a meal of tasty take-away knight! Can you tell which one of the numbered shadows has been cast by this dragon?

247 PILE UP

These piles of bricks aren't the random results of a child's play but clues to a final, at present blank, pile on the right. Like the rest, that one has six bricks each with a different one of the six letters. The numbers below the heaps tell you two things:
(a) The number of adjacent pairs of bricks in that column which also appear adjacent in the final pile.
(b) The number of adjacent pairs of bricks that make a correct pair but the wrong way up.
So:

would score one in the 'Correct' row if the final heap had an A directly above a C and a one in the 'Reversed' row if the final heap had a C on top of an A. From all this, can you create the final pile before it topples?

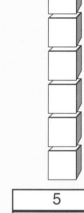

Correct	1	1	1	2	5
Reversed	0	0	0	0	0

248 SPOT THE DOG

Can you tell which of these happy hounds is the odd one out?

249 SET SQUARE

All the digits from 1 to 9 are used in this grid, but only once. Can you work out their positions in the grid and make the sums work? We've given two numbers to start you off.

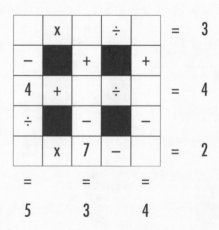

250 MAZE MYSTERY

Travel from the entrance to the exit of the maze, filling the path completely to create a picture.

251 SIX-PACK

By packing numbers in the empty spaces, can you make the numbers in each of the 16 hexagons add up to 25? No two numbers in each hexagon may be the same and you can't use zero. We've started you off.

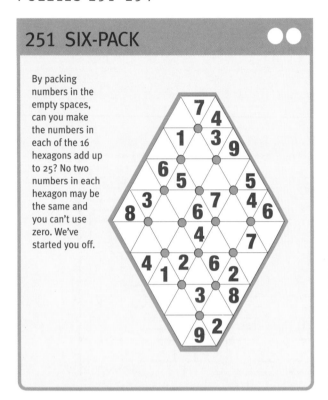

252 IT FIGURES

Place a number from 1 to 9 in each empty cell so that the sum of each vertical or horizontal block equals the number at the top or on the left of that block. Numbers may only be used once in each block.

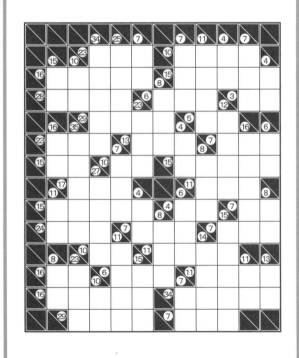

253 CELL STRUCTURE

The object is to create white areas surrounded by black walls, so that:
* Each white area contains only one number
* The number of cells in a white area is equal to the number in it
* The white areas are separated from each other with a black wall
* Cells containing numbers must not be filled in
* The black cells must be linked into a continuous wall
* Black cells cannot form a square of 2 x 2 or larger

	4		3			2		3
							6	
		2						
						2		
		5		2		4		
								2
		2		3				3
		3					3	
			2					
3							4	
					3			
			2					
		2						
	6				6		3	

254 LOST IN SPACE

Can you show this astronaut the way to his spaceship?

255 LOGISTICAL

At a recent 'point to point' horse-racing meeting in the country one of the most exciting events was the Ladies' Race. From the clues given below, can you work out in which order the five runners finished, and the name and occupation of the amateur jockey who rode each?

1 The doctor rode her mount into second place.

2 Di Richards didn't finish first, nor immediately in front of the secretary.

3 Captain Candy, which finished ahead of Drummer Boy, wasn't ridden by Sue Archer.

4 Lesley Carson, on Popcorn, finished immediately behind the vet.

5 Jane Piggott is a student at the local agricultural college.

6 The fifth horse to finish was the big grey called Snowstorm.

7 The woman who runs a farm isn't Vicky Mercer, whose horse brought her home in fourth place.

	Captain Candy	Drummer Boy	Eastern Star	Popcorn	Snowstorm	Di Richards	Jane Piggott	Lesley Carson	Sue Archer	Vicky Mercer	Farmer	Doctor	Secretary	Student	Vet
First															
Second															
Third															
Fourth															
Fifth															
Farmer															
Doctor															
Secretary															
Student															
Vet															
Di Richards															
Jane Piggott															
Lesley Carson															
Sue Archer															
Vicky Mercer															

Record in this grid all the information obtained from the clues, by using a cross to indicate a definite 'no' and a tick to show a definite 'yes'. Transfer these to all sections of the grid thus eliminating all but one possibility, which must be the correct one.

Place	Horse	Jockey	Occupation

256 GOLF LINK

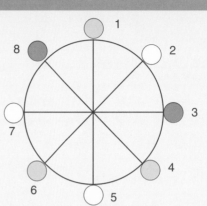

No.	Name	Shots	Prize
1			
2			
3			
4			
5			
6			
7			
8			

Eight people took part in a golf competition. Each person took his or her turn by standing on the tee, at the centre of a large circle, and putting a golf ball into one of the numbered holes. No two people putted the ball into the same hole and each person took a different number of shots to sink the ball into the hole he or she had chosen, the number of shots ranging from one to eight. In no case did the number of shots taken by a person match the number of the hole into which he or she putted the ball. Each person won a different prize. Gemma, who won the holiday vouchers, putted the ball into a white hole which was two counterclockwise of the hole at which the parasol was won. At the latter hole, two more shots were taken than at the former hole. Seven shots were taken to win the sombrero at a hole which was two clockwise of the hole at which John won his prize. Four shots were taken at a black hole, which was diametrically opposite the hole at which Jane won her prize.

The white hole at which the swimsuit was won was diametrically opposite the hole at which Mary won her prize. At the latter hole, six more shots were taken than at the former hole.

The greatest number of shots were taken to win the beachball, at a hole one counterclockwise of the black hole at which Edward won his prize. The number of shots taken to win the deckchair was more than the number of shots taken at the hole one counterclockwise of the hole at which the deckchair was won. Carol's hole had a higher number than Mike's. Donald won his prize at a hole whose number was half the number of the hole at which the beach towel (which was not Mike's prize) was won. One of the prizes won was a pair of sunglasses, and hole no. 8 was selected by a man.

Can you determine which person putted the ball into each hole, the prize each won and the number of shots taken by each?

257 INDEPENDENCE DAY

The twelve small squares each contain one of the letters or numbers making up the phrase USA 4 JULY, 1776. From the clues given below, can you place the correct number or letter in each of the squares?

Clues

1 Horizontal row B contains three numbers, but only one letter, which is not a vowel.

2 No letter or number occurs twice in any row or column.

3 The column in which a 7 appears immediately above the A is next right from the one containing the S, which is not the horizontal neighbour of either.

4 The L, which has a number in the square to its right, is in a square immediately above the 6.

5 One of the Us is immediately below the J, and immediately to the left of the 1.

6 Square A2 contains a number, and C4 contains a letter.

Letters: A; J; L; S; U; U; Y
Numbers: 1; 4; 6; 7; 7

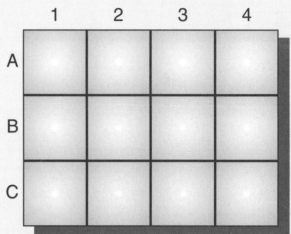

Starting tip: Begin by working out which is the letter in row B.

258 ZEROING IN

Twenty of the twenty-five squares in the diagram each contain a different one of the numbers 1 to 20, while each of the other five squares contains a zero. From the clues given below, can you place the correct number in each square? NB Where the phrase 'number' or 'single-digit number' occurs in a clue, this does not include zeros.

Clues

1 No row, column or diagonal (long or short) contains more than one zero.

2 The 19 in square B3 is the only two-digit number in that row, while the 7 is the only single-digit number in row 2.

3 The 9 is immediately below the 16, and immediately left of the 12.

4 The numbers in column E total 45, and those in row 2 total 51.

5 The number in A4 is five higher than the one in E5, which is itself one higher than the one in C2.

6 The 11 is immediately to the right of the 5 in row 4, while the 2 is to be found in a higher row than the 4.

7 The 17 appears in column D, somewhere below a zero, and somewhere above the 8.

8 The four numbers in column C are all even numbers, but do not include the 18.

9 The number 1 can be found in row 5, and the 6 in row 1.

10 The 10 is in the same column as the 3, but higher up.

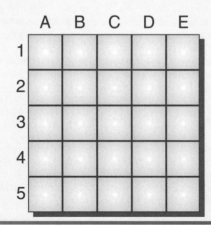

Starting tip: Begin by placing the 9.

259 LET'S FACE IT

Four children were each given a picture of a man's face, and invited to adorn it in a different manner. From the clues given below, can you work out the name and age of the child who was given each of pictures 1 to 4, and complete them by drawing in the missing detail in each picture?

Clues

1 Picture 2, which is clean-shaven, was produced by the artist a year older than Mary.

2 The oldest child produced picture 1.

3 Silas gave his character a monocle; this picture is somewhere to the right of the one produced by the artist aged 8.

4 Alistair is 9; his picture is not immediately to the right of the one with a moustache.

Name: ___ ___ ___ ___

Age: ___ ___ ___ ___

Feature: ___ ___ ___ ___

Names: Alistair; Jennifer; Mary; Silas
Ages: 8; 9; 10; 11
Features: beard; monocle; moustache; spectacles
Starting tip: Begin by naming the child aged 11.

260 IT FIGURES ●●●

Place a number from 1 to 9 in each empty cell so that the sum of each vertical or horizontal block equals the number at the top or on the left of that block. Numbers may only be used once in each block.

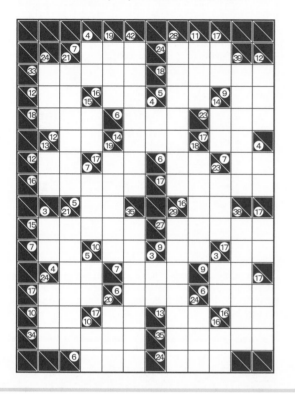

262 FOOT FAULT

Can you locate the eight differences between these two pictures?

261 TALK TURKEY ○

These crafty turkeys are avoiding Thanksgiving by hiding in the woods. How many can you see in this picture?

263 IT FIGURES ●●●

Place a number from 1 to 9 in each empty cell so that the sum of each vertical or horizontal block equals the number at the top or on the left of that block. Numbers may only be used once in each block.

264 LOGISTICAL

A new production of Shakespeare's *Measure For Measure* is being put on at a London theatre, and none of the five female parts in this play is being taken by a British actress. From the clues given, can you work out the full name of each actress, the part she's playing, and where she comes from?

	Atkinson	Byrne	Edmunds	Potter	Thornhill	Francisca	Isabella	Juliet	Mariana	Mistress Overdone	Australia	Canada	Eire	USA	Zimbabwe
Amanda															
Gail															
Melanie															
Susan															
Wilma															
Australia															
Canada															
Eire															
USA															
Zimbabwe															
Francisca															
Isabella															
Juliet															
Mariana															
Mistress Overdone															

Record in this grid all the information obtained from the clues, by using a cross to indicate a definite 'no' and a tick to show a definite 'yes'. Transfer these to all sections of the grid thus eliminating all but one possibility, which must be the correct one.

Forename	Surname	Role	Country

1 The actress playing Mistress Overdone, who comes from Eire, isn't Ms Atkinson.

2 Gail Thornhill isn't Canadian.

3 Miss Byrne, who comes from New York, isn't playing Francisca.

4 Miss Potter isn't playing Juliet, which isn't Susan's role either.

5 Amanda, who's appearing as Mariana, has a shorter surname than Wilma.

6 Both Melanie, the Zimbabwean actress, and the woman who's playing Francisca have surnames which begin with consonants.

265 IT FIGURES

Place a number from 1 to 9 in each empty cell so that the sum of each vertical or horizontal block equals the number at the top or on the left of that block. Numbers may only be used once in each block.

266 DOUBLE TROUBLE

Which of these two students are identical?

267 SWORD PLAY

Big Eric's in a spot of bother! He's invited Even Bigger Eric round for some sword-fighting practice, but he's lost the swords. How many can you find for him in the picture?

269 TAKE THREE

The numbered pictures each differ from picture A in three unique ways. Can you find these differences?

268 SNACK TIME

As Tommy walked down the street he met in fairly quick succession four of his friends, each of whom was eating something different. As it was a rather chilly day, each lad was wearing a sweater. From the clues given below, can you name each of the boys numbered 1 to 4 in the diagram in the order in which they were met, and say what coloured sweater each was wearing and what item each was eating?

Clues

1 Tommy met Kevin, who was wearing the blue sweater, some time later than he came across the lad who was eating a lollipop.

2 The boy in the beige sweater was the third friend Tommy met.

3 The youth eating a banana, who was not Simon, was encountered next after the one wearing the green sweater.

4 The lad in the red sweater, who was not Danny, was encountered some time after Lewis, whose snack was the chocolate bar.

Names: Danny; Kevin; Lewis; Simon
Sweaters: beige; blue; green; red
Snacks: apple; banana; chocolate bar; lollipop

Starting tip: First name the boy in the red sweater.

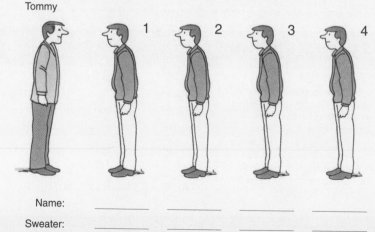

Name: _____ _____ _____ _____

Sweater: _____ _____ _____ _____

Snack: _____ _____ _____ _____

270 SET SQUARE ●●

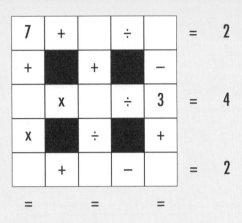

All the digits from 1 to 9 are used in this grid, but only once. Can you work out their positions in the grid and make the sums work? We've given two numbers to start you off.

271 SIX PACK ●●

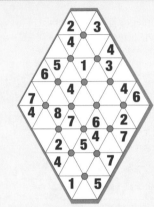

By inserting numbers in the empty spaces, can you make the numbers in each of the 1● hexagons add up to 25? No two numbers in each hexagon may be the same and you can't use zero. We've started you off.

272 DIGITAL TIME ●●

Place eight of the digits 1 to 9 once each in the squares so that multiplying the three in each line produces the number shown in the circle on the end.

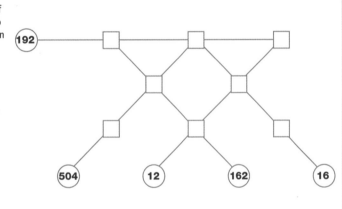

273 LOGIQUATIONS ●●

In the following problems the digits 0 to 9 are represented by letters. Within each separate puzzle the same letter always represents the same digit. Can you find the correct values each time so that all sums, both horizontal and vertical, are correct? There is a clue to help start you off.

ABCD	÷	D	=	EEEF
−		+		+
GHJF	−	DKJ	=	GGDK
JKDA	+	DKB	=	JJFH

A	B	C	D	E	F	G	H	J	K

Clue: JK ÷ KH = G

274 IT FIGURES ●●●

Place a number from 1 to 9 in each empty cell so that the sum of each vertical or horizontal block equals the number at the top or on the left of that block. Numbers may only be used once in each block.

275 LOGISTICAL

In Hollywood's heyday, Bitt Player was a character actor specializing in playing Latin types, and, though he never had a major role, he was seldom out of work. In one week he played scenes for five different movies; from the clues below, can you work out the nationality and occupation of the character he played each day, and say which film it was for?

Clues

1 It wasn't on Sunday (the first day of the week) that Bitt played an Italian.

2 The scene in which Bitt played a corrupt policeman was shot three days after the one for *The Storm*

3 Bitt played a dying soldier on Saturday.

4 On Friday, Bitt played a Spanish part, but not for *Dead End*.

5 It was for *Web Of Fear* that Bitt played a Brazilian.

6 Bitt's Mexican character was a bandit.

7 It was on an odd-numbered day of the week that Bitt took on the role of a sailor for *Hunted Man*; this wasn't the Greek character, who wasn't the one Bitt played on Wednesday.

	Brazilian	Greek	Italian	Mexican	Spanish	Bandit	Policeman	Sailor	Soldier	Waiter	Dead End	Hunted Man	Split Seconds	The Storm	Web Of Fear
Sunday															
Tuesday															
Wednesday															
Friday															
Saturday															
Dead End															
Hunted Man															
Split Seconds															
The Storm															
Web Of Fear															
Bandit															
Policeman															
Sailor															
Soldier															
Waiter															

Record in this grid all the information obtained from the clues, by using a cross to indicate a definite 'no' and a tick to show a definite 'yes'. Transfer these to all sections of the grid thus eliminating all but one possibility, which must be the correct one.

Working day	Role Nationality	Role Occupation	Film

276 TROMBONES

Which one of the numbered pictures has been developed from the negative of this trombone? Remember – in a negative, any area which is really white appears black, and any area which is really black appears white!

277 KNIGHT STUFF

There are eight differences between these two pictures – can you find them?

278 TRAIL BLAZING

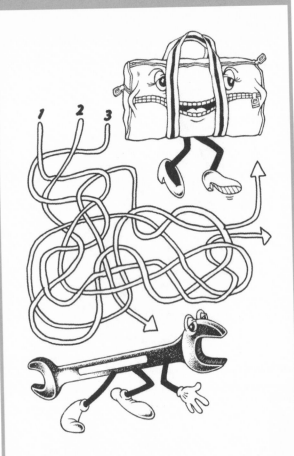

Can you tell which numbered trail will lead the toolbag to the wrench?

279 STAMPS OF VALUE

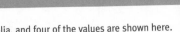

A new set of stamps has just been issued in Philatelia, and four of the values are shown here. From the clues given below, can you work out the design on each stamp, its face value, and the colour in which its frame and figures of value are printed?

Clues

1 The figure 5 does not appear in brown on any of the four stamps.
2 The stamp depicting the cathedral, which has a zero in its value panel, is shown immediately to the right of the stamp with a brown frame.
3 Stamp 4 has a 1 in its value panel, while the harbour is not the design featured on stamp 3.
4 The 15 cents stamp is shown in a position directly above or below the blue one.
5 The stamp with the red frame bears the value next higher than the one depicting the mountains, which is not in position 1.

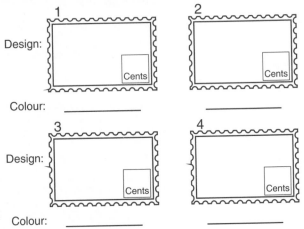

Designs: cathedral; harbour; mountains; waterfall
Values: 10 cents; 15 cents; 25 cents; 50 cents
Colours: blue; brown; green; red

Starting tip: Begin by working out the value on the brown stamp.

280 LOGISTICAL

Five women have each built up an extensive collection of pottery figurines of different creatures. From the clues below, can you work out each collector's full name, the type of figure she collects, and how many she has amassed?

Clues

1 It isn't Mrs Iveagh who has collected 91 pottery dogs of different breeds and sizes.
2 The cat-collector hasn't accumulated exactly 79 of them.
3 It's Ms Wallace who has collected 118 figurines, and Mrs Tate who collects pottery teddy-bears.
4 Janet is very proud of her collection of dragons.
5 Monica has the smallest collection, but it isn't Veronica who has the largest; Mrs Hayward has more than one hundred figurines displayed in the front room of the home.
6 Cynthia's surname is Iveagh; Ruth doesn't collect cats.

Forename	Surname	Figurine	Number

	Courtauld	Hayward	Iveagh	Tate	Wallace	Cats	Dogs	Dragons	Pigs	Teddy-bears	63	79	91	107	118
Cynthia															
Janet															
Monica															
Ruth															
Veronica															
63															
79															
91															
107															
118															
Cats															
Dogs															
Dragons															
Pigs															
Teddy-bears															

Record in this grid all the information obtained from the clues, by using a cross to indicate a definite 'no' and a tic to show a definite 'yes'. Transfer these to all sections of the grid thus eliminating all but one possibility, which must be the correct one.

281 MAZE MYSTERY

Travel from the entrance to the exit of the maze, filling the path completely to create a picture.

282 ROMEO AND JULIET

See if you can help Romeo reach Juliet by finding a path through this maze, from start to finish.

283 SIX-PACK

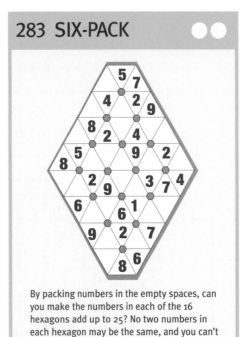

By packing numbers in the empty spaces, can you make the numbers in each of the 16 hexagons add up to 25? No two numbers in each hexagon may be the same, and you can't use zero. We've started you off.

284 SET SQUARE

All the digits from 1 to 9 are used in this grid, but only once each. Can you work out their positions in the grid and make the sums work? We've given two numbers to start you off.

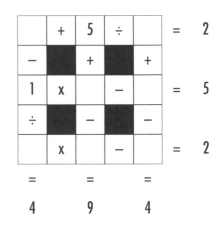

285 WHATEVER NEXT?

Which two numbers continue this sequence?

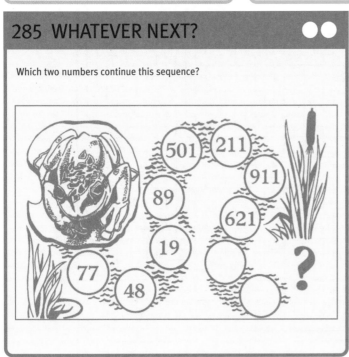

286 TOTTERING TOWERS

These piles of bricks aren't the random results of child's play but clues to the final, at present, blank tower on the right. Like the rest, that tower has one brick in each of the six colours.

The numbers below each heap tell you two things:
(a) How many adjacent pairs of bricks are actually correct in the final tower.
(b) How many adjacent pairs of bricks make a correct pair but the wrong way up.

So:

would score one on the first number if the final tower had green directly above yellow. It would score one on the second number if the final tower had yellow on top of green.

From all of this, can you create the tower before it finally topples?

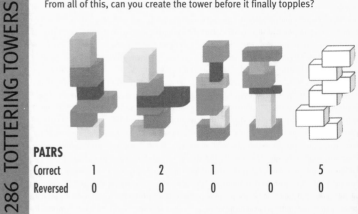

PAIRS

Correct	1	2	1	1	5
Reversed	0	0	0	0	0

287 LOGISTICAL

At a craft fair in the village hall, five large and impressive matchstick models were on display, each having been painstakingly constructed by a local person. From the clues given below, can you work out which model was made by which man, and can you also determine how many matches were used and how much time was taken to build each object?

Clues

1 Derek Burns took less than five months to construct his windmill.

2 Charlie Head used more matchsticks than any of the other four men, but his was not the model that took the greatest number of months to build.

3 The cathedral is made up of just 4,000 matchsticks, which is more than were used to construct the steam-roller.

4 The model that was built in exactly four months comprises just 3,500 matchsticks, which is fewer matchsticks than were used by Alec Wood.

5 Brian Box took just two months to complete his model and used more than 3,000 matchsticks to do so.

6 The Ferris wheel was built in just three months and is made up of fewer than 5,000 matchsticks.

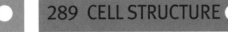
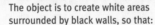

	Alec Wood	Brian Box	Charlie Head	Derek Burns	Eric Striker	3,000 matches	3,500 matches	4,000 matches	4,500 matches	5,000 matches	Two months	Three months	Four months	Six months	Seven months
Cathedral															
Ferris wheel															
Ship															
Steam-roller															
Windmill															
Two months										
Three months										
Four months										
Six months										
Seven months										
3,000 matches					
3,500 matches					
4,000 matches					
4,500 matches					
5,000 matches					

Model	Maker	No. of matches	Time taken

Record in this grid all the information obtained from the clues, by using a cross to indicate a definite 'no' and a tick to show a definite 'yes'. Transfer these to all sections of the grid thus eliminating all but one possibility, which must be the correct one.

288 SMILE PLEASE

The top left-hand picture of this face is complete, but all the others have at least one detail missing. Can you add the missing details to make all the pictures the same?

289 CELL STRUCTURE

The object is to create white areas surrounded by black walls, so that:
* Each white area contains only one number
* The number of cells in a white area is equal to the number in it.
* The white areas are separated from each other with a black wall.
* Cells containing numbers must not be filled in.
* The black cells must be linked into a continuous wall.
* Black cells cannot form a square of 2 x 2 or larger.

9	3			5				
					6			
5								
3			4		3			
						1		4
3		1						
		4		5				9
								7
		7						
		3			2		1	

290 STAMP DUTY

Which of these numbered prints was made by the stamp featured here?

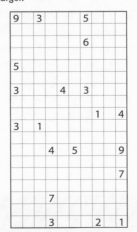

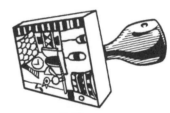

291 EASTER BUNNY

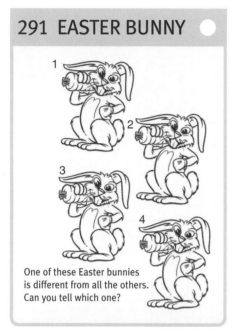

One of these Easter bunnies is different from all the others. Can you tell which one?

292 PARROT PIECES

These nine pieces can be fitted together to make a complete outline of the parrot, but three of the pieces are slightly wrong. Can you see which three they are?

293 RAT'S TRAIL

Can you help this rat find its way to the cheese?

294 PILE UP

These piles of bricks aren't the random results of a child's play but clues to a final, at present blank, pile on the right. Like the rest, that one has six bricks each with a different one of the six letters. The numbers below the heaps tell you two things:

(a) The number of adjacent pairs of bricks in that column which also appear adjacent in the final pile.

(b) The number of adjacent pairs of bricks that make a correct pair but the wrong way up.

So:

would score one in the 'Correct' row if the final heap had an A directly above a C and a one in the 'Reversed' row if the final heap had a C on top of an A. From all this, can you create the final pile before it topples?

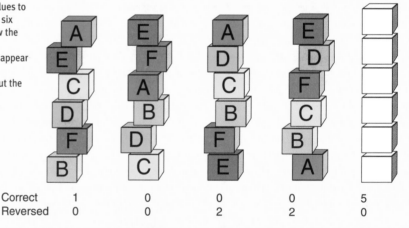

Correct	1	0	0	0	5
Reversed	0	0	2	2	0

295 SET SQUARE

All the digits from 1 to 9 are used in this grid, but only once. Can you work out their positions in the grid and make the sums work? We've given two numbers to start you off.

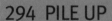

296 SET SQUARE

All the digits from 1 to 9 are used in this grid, but only once each. Can you work out their positions in the grid and make the sums work? We've given two numbers to start you off.

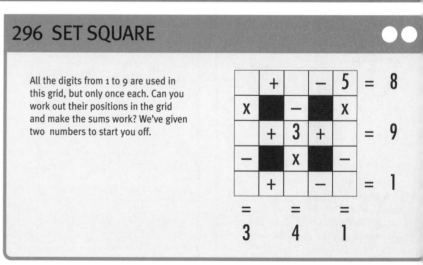

297 LOGISTICAL

In a new science fiction movie, some of the main characters are a family of robots, identical except for the colours of their casings. From the clues below, can you work out the colour of each robot's casing, and the full name of the actor who's inside it?

Clues

1 The actor who plays 'Roxanne', who does not have a four-letter surname, isn't Phil.
2 The yellow robot is played by the actor surnamed Jenkins, while the one called Marvin appears as 'Ramona'.
3 Claudia, whose surname isn't Link, appears in the movie as the silver robot, which has a male name.
4 'Romulus', the robot played by Selena, doesn't have a green casing.
5 George's surname is Krag.
6 'Remus' is the robot with the red casing.

Record in this grid all the information obtained from the clues, by using a cross to indicate a definite 'no' and a tick to show a definite 'yes'. Transfer these to all sections of the grid thus eliminating all but one possibility, which must be the correct one.

Robot	Colour	Forename	Surname

298 LOGISTICAL

Five children who lived in Softwood Cuttings were allowed a few square feet in which to grow their own choice of seeds. From the information given, can you work out their full names, plot area and variety of seeds?

Clues

1 One boy intended to sell his 7 square feet of rocket leaves to the local supermarket, while Martine was looking forward to eating all her radishes.
2 Kylie's plot was twice as big as Dibber's poppy garden.
3 Shovell's area was larger than Jack's but smaller than the candytuft.
4 Miss Potts' flowers occupied an area of 4 square feet.
5 Dean's surname wasn't Trowell.

Record in this grid all the information obtained from the clues, by using a cross to indicate a definite 'no' and a tick to show a definite 'yes'. Transfer these to all sections of the grid thus eliminating all but one possibility, which must be the correct one.

First name	Surname	Plot area	Seed type

299 SPACE CHASE

This astronaut doesn't like the idea of becoming a spaceman sandwich, so he's clearing off back to his rocket! He wishes he could find his stun-gun. How many stun-guns can you find in this picture?

300 TENT FLAP

Which of the lettered paths will lead this confused camper back to his tent?

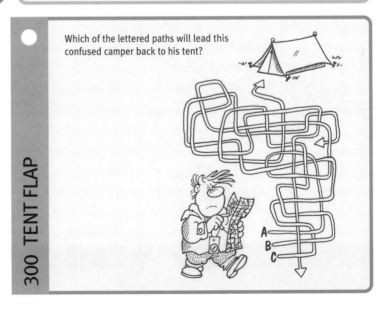

301 CELL STRUCTURE

The object is to create white areas surrounded by black walls, so that:
- Each white area contains only one number
- The number of cells in a white area is equal to the number in it
- The white areas are separated from each other with a black wall
- Cells containing numbers must not be filled in
- The black cells must be linked into a continuous wall
- Black cells cannot form a square of 2x2 or larger

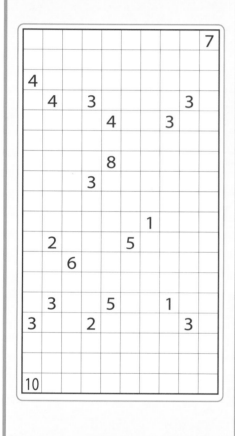

302 SIX-PACK

By packing numbers in the empty spaces, can you make the numbers in each of the 16 hexagons add up to 25? No two numbers in each hexagon may be the same and you can't use zero. We've started you off.

303 DARTING ABOUT

A dart player scores 60 with three darts hitting a treble, a double and a single (no bulls). Given that the three numbers that he hits add up to 31 and that the difference between the largest and smallest numbers is 11, can you work out how his score is made up?

304 STRIP TRICK

In what order must the five pieces below be arranged to form the complete strip shown above?

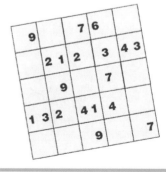

305 PARTY TIME

If it happens to be true that:
MONDAY = TODAY
TUESDAY = JUNE DAY
SUNDAY = THURSDAY
FRIDAY = BIRTHDAY
Then what day was yesterday?

306 IT'S MAGIC

Can you complete this Magic Square so that every row, column and diagonal adds up to the magic total? To help you we have placed figures above 5 in rows 1, 3, 5 and figures below 5 in rows 2 & 4.

HINT: Every row has units 1, 3, 5, 7, 9 once.

9		7 6		
	2 1 2		3	4 3
		9	7	
1 3 2		4 1 4		
		9		7

13	15	17	19	21
23	25	27	29	31
33	35	37	39	41
43	45	47	49	51
53	55	57	59	61

307 LOGIQUATIONS

In the following problems the digits 0 to 9 are represented by letters. Within each separate puzzle the same letter always represents the same digit. Can you find the correct values each time so that all sums, both horizontal and vertical, are correct? There is a clue to help start you off.

$$
\begin{array}{ccc}
AB & \times \; CD & = DBEB \\
+ & + & - \\
\underline{FGHJ} & + \; \underline{FHJE} & = \underline{EGEC} \\
FFCD & + \; BGFH & = EFHK
\end{array}
$$

A	B	C	D	E	F	G	H	J	K

CLUE: 2 X FD = EB

308 WHATEVER NEXT?

Which two numbers continue this sequence?

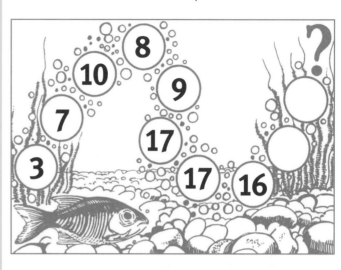

309 IN THE MAIL

Four housewife neighbours in a suburban area of an American town each had a different coloured mailbox at the entrance to their property. From the clues given below, can you work out the name of the woman who lives at each address, and work out the colour of her mailbox?

Clues
1 The green mailbox is next to Gemma's on one side, and Mrs Gerber's on the other.
2 Arlene chose the yellow mailbox for her gate, at a house with a higher number than Mrs Fishbein's.
3 The red mailbox is at Mrs Baron's house.
4 The blue mailbox is on the gate of number 232, which is not Louise's home.

First names: Arlene; Gemma; Kate; Louise
Surnames: Baron; Fishbein; Flint; Gerber
Mailboxes: blue; green; red; yellow

Starting tip: Begin by placing the green mailbox.

228   **230**   **232**   **234**

First name: _____ _____ _____ _____
Surname: _____ _____ _____ _____
Colour: _____ _____ _____ _____

310 GAME ON

What game is involved here?

JZQONU   LHKDR   ROZRRJX   EHRGDQ   JZROZQNU

311 SPOT THE DIFFERENCE

One of these scruffy birds is different from the rest. Can you tell which?

312 IT FIGURES

Place a number from 1 to 9 in each empty cell so that the sum of each vertical or horizontal block equals the number at the top or on the left of that block. Numbers may only be used once in each block.

314 WEIGHED UP

Hats must be in heavy wool this year and the snow fall is light! As you can see, two sets of seesaws in the park balance beautifully. How many hats are needed to make the third seesaw level?

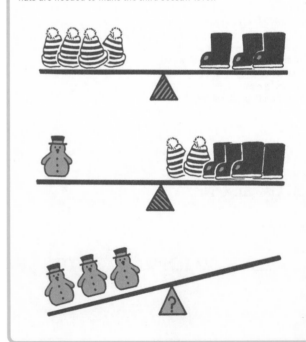

313 ISLAND HOPPING

Each circle containing a number represents an island. The object is to connect each island with vertical or horizontal bridges so that:
• The number of bridges is the same as the number inside the island.
• There can be up to two bridges between two islands.
• Bridges cannot cross islands or other bridges.
• There is a continuous path connecting all the islands.

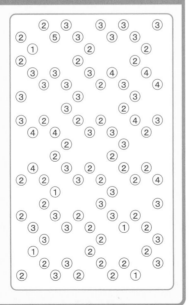

315 TELL THE UNTRUTH

The four girls depicted in the diagram are all, I'm afraid, inveterate little liars. From the clues given below, bearing in mind that every statement they make is untrue, can you correctly name the girl in each position, work out her true age, and describe the pet she owns?

Clues
1. Jenny says, "Hello, I'm nine, and I'm sitting in position 4."
2. Josie says, "Hi, I'm sitting next to my friend whose pet is a cat."
3. Jemima says, "Hello, I'm sitting next to Julie, whose pet is a tortoise, and my friend who owns the cat is nine."
4. Julie says, "Hi, my pet is the budgie, and I'm eight years old. I'm in position 2 in the line."
5. To help you out, we'll tell you that the girl aged 10 is in position 3, Josie's pet is a puppy, and the girl numbered 4 in the diagram has a budgie.

Names: Jemima; Jenny; Josie; Julie
Ages: 8; 9; 10;11
Pets: budgie; cat; puppy; tortoise

Starting tip: Begin by identifying Julie's pet.

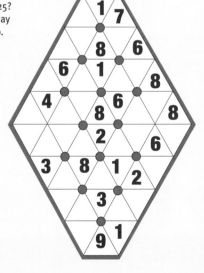

Name: _____ _____ _____ _____

Age: _____ _____ _____ _____

Pet: _____ _____ _____ _____

317 SIX-PACK

By packing numbers in the empty spaces, can you make the numbers in each of the 16 hexagons add up to 25? No two numbers in each hexagon may be the same, and you can't use zero. We've started you off.

316 NEGATIVE

In a negative, everything which is really white appears black and everything which is really black appears white. Can you tell which one of the six karate experts is shown as a negative in the top left-hand corner?

318 DOT-TO-DOT

Join the dots from 1 to 31 to reveal the hidden picture.

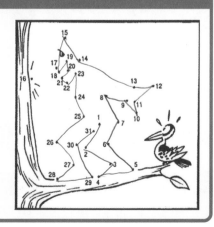

319 WEB MAZE

See if you can find a path through this web which will lead one spider to the other.

320 VIVE LA FRANCE

Each of the seventeen squares in the figure in the diagram contains one of the letters which form the name NAPOLEON BONAPARTE, in recognition of the French Fête Nationale celebrated on July 14. From the clues given below, can you insert all seventeen letters in their correct squares?

Clues

1 None of the letters which occur more than once in the name is immediately adjacent in any direction, including diagonally, to one of its duplicates.

2 The letter in the centre of the middle row is T; it has a consonant directly above it.

3 The diagonal sequence O P A appears somewhere in the layout reading downwards from right to left.

4 Neither of the two end squares of the middle row contains a vowel.

5 The letters at the left-hand end of both the top and bottom rows are identical.

6 The three As are all in different rows, and two of them have an N diagonally immediately above and to the left of them.

7 Both Es are in the same row.

8 The pairing N P occurs in one of the rows, reading left to right.

9 None of the columns reading downwards forms an English three-letter word.

10 The L, which has a consonant as its right-hand neighbour, is in the row above the B.

Letters to be inserted: A; A; A; B; E; E; L; N; N; N; O; O; O; P; P; R; T

Starting tip: Begin by placing the sequence referred to in clue 3.

321 SQUARING THE CIRCLE

What, logically, comes next?

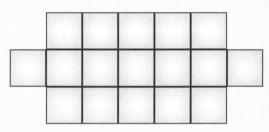

322 FREAK CONVERSION

Can you find the unique fraction

$$\frac{AB}{BC}$$

which when converted to a decimal

$$= 0.BCA ?$$

323 MAZE

Can you find a path through this maze?

START

FINISH

324 DARTING ABOUT

A dart player scored 91 with three darts hitting a treble, a double and a single (no bulls). Given that the three numbers that he hits add up to 47 and that the difference between the largest and smallest numbers is 5 can you work out how his score is made up?

Treble   Double   Single

325 ON THE FLY

One day, a young Biggles took Algy on a training flight round a square course. On the first leg they averaged 100mph: on the second leg 200 mph. Gaining confidence, they did the third leg at 300mph and finished with a strut-shattering 400mph along the last leg. Algy reckons their average speed for the whole journey must be 250mph. Is he right?

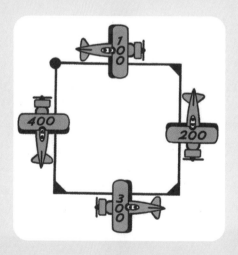

326 WEIGHED UP

How many cats are needed to balance the bottom set of scales?

327 BATTLE ZONE

Each of the figures shown differs slightly from the other three in one small detail. Can you spot all four extra details?

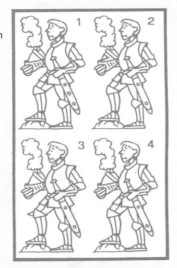

328 SPIDER SCARE

There's nothing Clarissa hates more than big spiders – except for even bigger spiders, of course! Which two pictures of Clarissa are exactly the same?

329 A BOX IN THE SHED

When Joe needed something for a job about the house, he would say "They're in a box in the shed". The four boxes shown in the diagram standing next to each other on a shelf, all of different colours, each contain a different number of useful items. From the clues given below, can you work out the full details?

Clues
1 The 43 nails of assorted sizes are not in the brown box.
2 There are 58 items in the blue box.
3 The screws are in the green box, one of whose immediate neighbours on the shelf contains the washers, and the other the largest number of items.
4 The carpet tacks are in box C.

Box colours: blue; brown; green; red
Number: 39; 43; 58; 65
Items: carpet tacks; nails; screws; washers

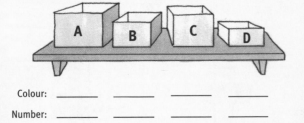

Colour: ____ ____ ____ ____

Number: ____ ____ ____ ____

Items: ____ ____ ____ ____

Starting tip: First work out the colour of the box containing the nails.

330 SIX-PACK

By packing numbers in the empty spaces, can you make the numbers in each of the 16 hexagons add up to 25? No two numbers in each hexagon may be the same and you can't use zero. We've started you off.

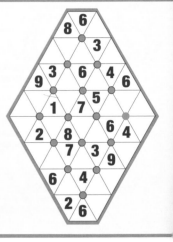

331 ALL CHANGE

At the height of Victorian England a lady of quality could only enjoy seaside bathing by hiring a bathing-machine from which she could descend modestly into the water wearing an ankle-length one-piece bathing dress. This problem features four such machines. From the clues given below, can you fully identify the lady who changed in each machine, and work out the colour of the striped bathing-costume in which she stepped into the sea?

Clues

1 Bertha's machine was immediately to the right of the one used by Miss Marchbanks.
2 Machine C was the one Miss Langthorpe hired.
3 Miss Carstairs wore the green and white striped costume.
4 Euphemia Ponsonby used a machine separated from the one whose occupant wore the orange and white bathing suit only by the one hired by Lavinia.
5 It was in machine B that one lady changed into her red and white bathing-costume.

First names: Bertha; Euphemia; Lavinia; Victoria
Surnames: Carstairs; Langthorpe; Marchbanks; Ponsonby
Costumes: blue and white; green and white; orange and white; red and white

First name: _____ _____ _____ _____

Surname: _____ _____ _____ _____

Costume: _____ _____ _____ _____

Starting tip: Start by working out the first name of the lady who hired machine D.

332 IT FIGURES

Place a number from 1 to 9 in each empty cell so that the sum of each vertical or horizontal block equals the number at the top or on the left of that block. Numbers may only be used once in each block.

333 DOT-TO-DOT

Join the dots from 1 to 46 to reveal the hidden picture.

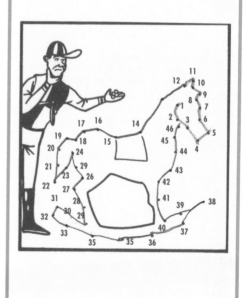

334 SILHOUETTE

Shade in every fragment containing a dot – and what have you got?

335 ACES HIGH

The four bridge players sitting round the table each had the Ace of a different suit in his or her hand on the deal in question. From the clues given below, can you fully identify the player in each of the four seats, and work out which Ace each holds? NB North and South play as partners against East and West.

Clues
1 Richard's Ace was the same colour as the one held by Ruff, who was in the North seat.
2 Martina's partner was holding the Ace of Hearts.
3 The woman sitting West, whose surname is not Tenace, had the Ace of Spades.
4 Paul Hand was partnering Esther.
5 The Ace of Clubs was not held by the player sitting South.

First names: Esther; Martina; Paul; Richard
Surnames: Hand; Ruff; Tenace; Trick
Aces: Clubs; Diamonds; Hearts; Spades

First name: _____
Surname: _____
Ace: _____

First name: _____
Surname: _____
Ace: _____

First name: _____
Surname: _____
Ace: _____

First name: _____
Surname: _____
Ace: _____

Starting tip: Begin by working out which Ace Richard held.

338 SIX-PACK

By packing numbers in the empty spaces, can you make the numbers in each of the 16 hexagons add up to 25? No two numbers in each hexagon may be the same and you can't use zero. We've started you off.

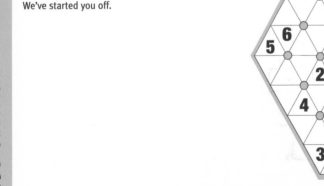

336 TRIO

Which three vases are identical?

337 BLACK OUT

Can you decide which two of the ten stereos are shown in silhouette at the top?

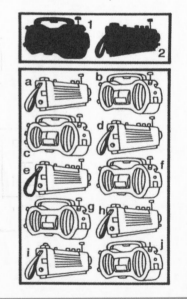

339 MAZE MYSTERY

Travel from the entrance to the exit of the maze, filling the path completely to create a picture.

340 SILHOUETTE

Shade in every fragment containing a dot – and what have you got?

342 ISLAND HOPPING

Each circle containing a number represents an island. The object is to connect each island with vertical or horizontal bridges so that:
• The number of bridges is the same as the number inside the island.
• There can be up to two bridges between two islands.
• Bridges cannot cross islands or other bridges.
• There is a continuous path connecting all the islands.

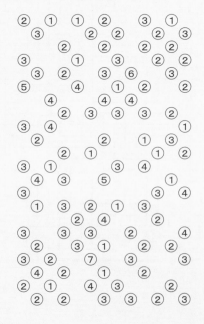

341 IN THE STALLS

The four central seats in each of the first three rows of the stalls at the theatre were all occupied at a recent performance. From the clues given below, can you place each of the listed people in their correct seats?

Clues
1 Peter was sitting directly behind Angela, and somewhere diagonally in front of Henry.
2 Nina had the ticket for seat 12 in row B.
3 The four seats featured in each row are occupied by two males and two females.
4 Maxine is two places to the right of Robert in the same row of the stalls.
5 Judy, who is immediately behind Charles, has her husband Vincent as her right-hand neighbour.
6 One of the men in the audience is sitting in seat 13 of row A.
7 Tony, Janet and Lydia all have seats in different rows of the stalls, the latter having a male neighbour to her left.

Names: Angela; Charles; Henry; Janet; Judy; Lydia; Maxine; Nina; Peter; Robert; Tony; Vincent

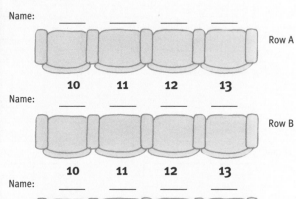

Name: _____ _____ _____ _____   Row A

      10   **11**   **12**   **13**

Name: _____ _____ _____ _____   Row B

      10   **11**   **12**   **13**

Name: _____ _____ _____ _____   Row C

      10   **11**   **12**   **13**

Starting tip: Begin by naming the man in seat 13 of row A.

343 DARTING ABOUT

A dart player scores 66 with three darts hitting a treble, a double and a single (no bulls). Given that the three numbers that he hits add up to 31 and that the difference between the largest and smallest numbers is 10 can you work out how his score is made up?

Treble   **Double**   **Single**

344 CELL STRUCTURE

The object is to create white areas surrounded by black walls, so that:
• Each white area contains only one number
• The number of cells in a white area is equal to the number in it
• The white areas are separated from each other with a black wall
• Cells containing numbers must not be filled in
• The black cells must be linked into a continuous wall
• Black cells cannot form a square of 2 x 2 or larger

3						
		3		3		
1						
				3		
	2					
					9	
1		5				
		9				
					6	4
3	5		10			
9						
		5				
						4

345 DON'T PAY THE PIPER...

The diagram shows the Pied Piper leading away the children of Hamelin after the town refused to pay him for ridding it of rats. From the clues given below, can you name the first four children in the line, work out their ages, and say what work their father does in the town?

Clues
1 The cowherd's child is directly behind six-year-old Gretchen as they follow the Piper.
2 Hans is younger than Johann.
3 The boy who leads the line is not immediately followed by the butcher's child.
4 The child aged seven is number 3 in the line.
5 Maria, whose father is an apothecary, is younger than the child in position 2.

Names: Gretchen; Hans; Johann; Maria
Ages: 5; 6; 7; 8
Fathers: apothecary; butcher; cowherd; woodcutter

Name: ___ ___ ___ ___
Age: ___ ___ ___ ___
Father: ___ ___ ___ ___

Starting tip: Start by placing Gretchen.

346 SIX-PACK

By packing numbers in the empty spaces, can you make the numbers in each of the 16 hexagons add up to 25? No two numbers in each hexagon may be the same and you can't use zero. We've started you off.

347 MAZE MYSTERY

Travel from the entrance to the exit of the maze, filling the path completely to create a picture.

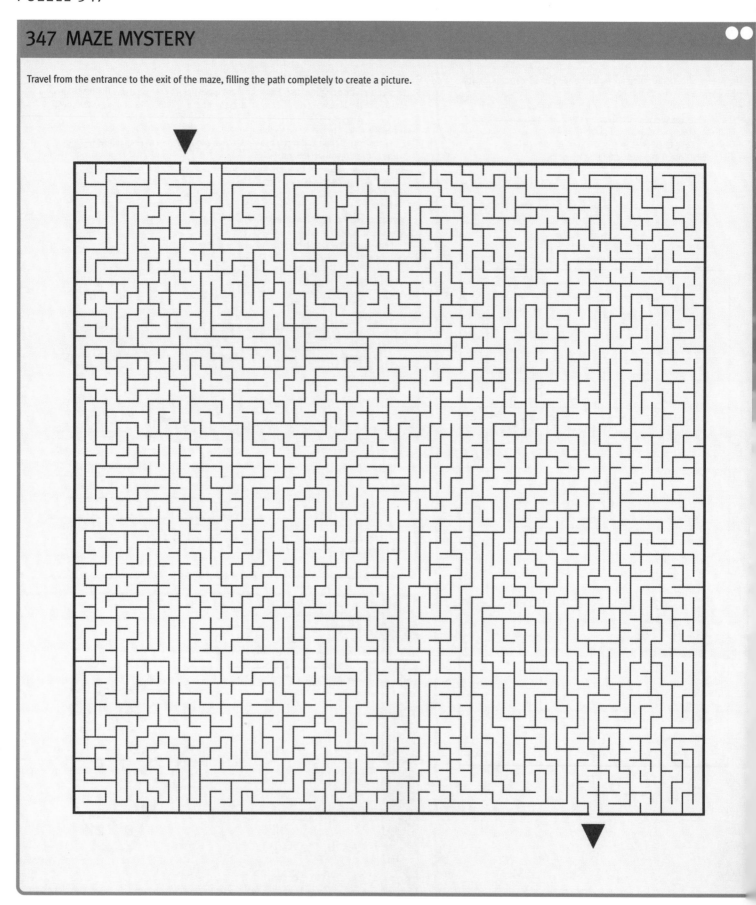

Pandora Persimmons is the presenter of a quiz show in which successful contestants earn the right to open one of the boxes displayed as in the diagram, the contents of which may prove to be worth having or virtually worthless. Pandora tempts the contestants to forfeit the right to open by offering sums of money, which, in this instance, were refused. From the clues given below, can you indicate in the diagram in what order each of our six qualified to open a box, which box each chose and what it contained?

Clues

1 The order of the contestants did not tally with the number of the box each chose to open.

2 Lynne, who opened box 2, won a cash prize but less than that won by Sharon, whose turn was more than one earlier.

3 Michael, whose turn was next after that of the winner of $100, opened a box more than one place further right than the winner's.

4 The box containing the bar of soap turned out to be next left to the one opened by the fifth contestant; the box chosen by Jim was further left than either.

5 The turn of the contestant who collected the wooden spoon was next before that of the one who was less than ecstatic at winning 50 cents; the box with the spoon in it was next right to the one holding $1,000.

6 Susan opened the box next right to that chosen by Rob, whose turn immediately followed hers.

7 No two men opened adjacent boxes; the winner of the star prize of $5,000 was the only person whose box was between a man's, on the left, and a woman's, on the right.

Contestants: Jim; Lynne; Michael; Rob; Sharon; Susan
Contents: 50 cents; $100; $1,000; $5,000; bar of soap; wooden spoon

Name: _____ _____ _____ _____ _____ _____

Order: _____ _____ _____ _____ _____ _____

Prize: _____ _____ _____ _____ _____ _____

Starting tip: Work out in which box the $5,000 was hidden.

348 PANDORA'S BOXES

---

349 DICEY BUSINESS

In order to answer that all-important social question, how many flies are there round the grease spot, six dice are thrown. The answers to the first three throws are given. So what is the answer for the fourth throw?

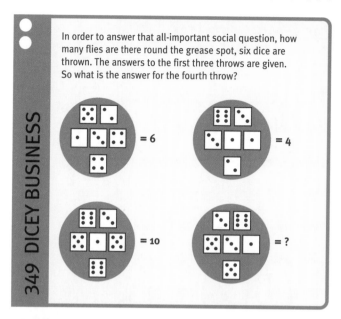

= 6

= 4

= 10

= ?

---

350 GUYS IN THE BLACK HATS

The four posters on the wall of the Sheriff's office in the Wild West town of Redrock show the members of the notorious Black Hat Gang of train-robbers. From the clues given below, can you fill in on the drawing each outlaw's forename, nickname and surname?

Clues

1 Herbert's picture is horizontally adjacent to that of 'Butch' McColl.

2 Poster A shows Jacob, but Silvester Jaggard isn't depicted on poster C.

3 The poster with a picture of the man surnamed Wolf is horizontally adjacent to the one which shows the one nicknamed 'Pony'.

4 Churchman, who appears on poster D, isn't the outlaw nicknamed 'Apache'.

First names: Herbert; Jacob; Matthew; Silvester
Nicknames: 'Apache'; 'Butch'; 'Pony'; 'Rio'
Surnames: Churchman; Jaggard; McColl; Wolf

First name: _____ A **WANTED**   **WANTED** B
Nickname: _____
Surname: _____   _____

First name: _____ C **WANTED**   **WANTED** D
Nickname: _____
Surname: _____   _____

Starting tip: Work out the first name of the baddie on poster C.

By packing numbers in the empty spaces, can you make the numbers in each of the 16 hexagons add up to 25? No two numbers in each hexagon may be the same and you can't use zero. We've started you off.

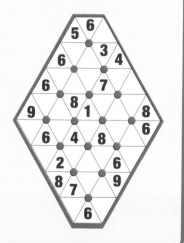

351 SIX-PACK

352 MIRROR IMAGE

There are four pairs of mirror images below. Can you identify the pairs, and find the odd-one-out?

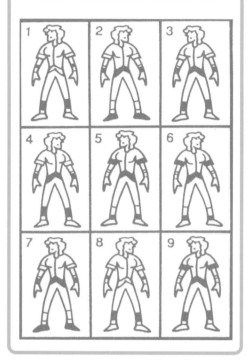

354 TWIN SET

Two of the pictures below are identical. Can you spot the 'twins' and identify what is different about the two remaining pictures?

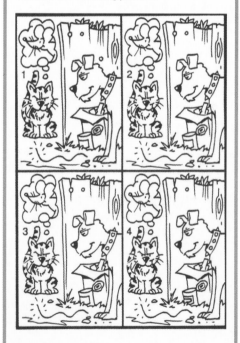

353 ALL SQUARE

A garden square in the city centre has a large hotel occupying each of its sides, as shown numbered 1 to 4 in the diagram. From the clues given below, can you name each hotel and its manager, and say how many rooms it boasts?

Clues

1 The hotel run by Max is directly across the square from the Majestic, which has more rooms, and which is not managed by Rupert.
2 The hotel on the western side of the square does not have 203 rooms.
3 The hotel with the fewest rooms occupies the north side of the square.
4 Guy runs the Castle Hotel, which is next counterclockwise round the square from the one with 197 rooms.
5 Perry is the manager of the hotel numbered 3 on the plan, which has fewer rooms than the Excelsior.

Hotels: Castle; Excelsior; Grand; Majestic
Managers: Guy; Max; Perry; Rupert
Rooms: 158; 197; 203; 224

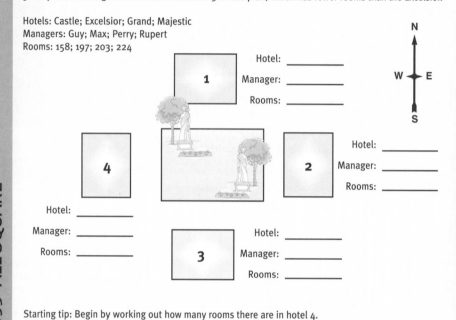

Starting tip: Begin by working out how many rooms there are in hotel 4.

355 UNLUCKY FOR SOME

Each of the white squares in the diagram contains a different one of the numbers 1 to 13. From the clues given below, can you place the correct number in each of the squares?

Clues

1 There are no two-digit numbers in rows A or D, or in columns 1 or 4.
2 The 9 does not occupy a corner square.
3 The 6 is in direct line below the 2.
4 The number in E5 is one below the one in A3.
5 The 1 is diagonally below and to the left of the 12, and diagonally above and to the right of the 10.
6 The number in square B4 is two higher than the one in square D2.
7 The 8 is in direct line above the number 13.

Numbers: 1; 2; 3; 4; 5; 6; 7; 8; 9; 10; 11; 12; 13

Starting tip: Start by placing the 1 in its correct position.

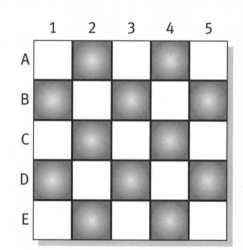

356 MAZE MYSTERY

Travel from the entrance to the exit of the maze, filling the path completely to create a picture.

357 COFFIN'S CANOE

This extraordinary little puzzle was made by Stuart Coffin – a world-renowned puzzle craftsman. The 'canoe' has two recesses, one at each end, into which the balls will fit. A divider separates the two balls. If you think that the problem of rolling balls into the holes is just too easy, let us point out that you must pop them into place *simultaneously*! Now that might seem impossible – but it can be done. How?

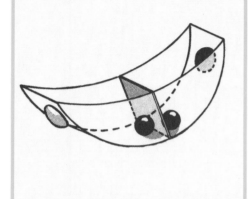

359 KNOT SO

Which of the tangled ropes below will form a knot, and which will not?

358 JOB IN HAND

Although it's a quiet time for building works, these five merchants are busy supplying the needs of five builders who each need a different item for a different project.

Can you put the facts into place?

1 Alf Pryce is calling at Hodsup who do not sell stone but he does not want wood which is for the conservatory which is not being built by A Cowerboy.
2 T Brakes wants sand.
3 The ballast is for the path. Cy Berman is building a bungalow.
4 The customer at BricksRus is building a garage but this is not Val Heegham or A Cowerboy and none of these three wants cement or stone.
5 Neither Just Slates nor Mortar Mart sells stone and the latter does not supply wood.

PRODUCT	CUSTOMER	ITEM	JOB
BRICKSRUS	A COWERBOY	BALLAST	BUNGALOW
	ALF PRYCE	CEMENT	CONSERVATORY
	CY BERMAN	SAND	GARAGE
	T BRAKES	STONE	PATH
	VAL HEEGHAM	WOOD	WALL
HIRAN HIRE	A COWERBOY	BALLAST	BUNGALOW
	ALF PRYCE	CEMENT	CONSERVATORY
	CY BERMAN	SAND	GARAGE
	T BRAKES	STONE	PATH
	VAL HEEGHAM	WOOD	WALL
HODSUP	A COWERBOY	BALLAST	BUNGALOW
	ALF PRYCE	CEMENT	CONSERVATORY
	CY BERMAN	SAND	GARAGE
	T BRAKES	STONE	PATH
	VAL HEEGHAM	WOOD	WALL
JUST SLATES	A COWERBOY	BALLAST	BUNGALOW
	ALF PRYCE	CEMENT	CONSERVATORY
	CY BERMAN	SAND	GARAGE
	T BRAKES	STONE	PATH
	VAL HEEGHAM	WOOD	WALL
MORTAR MART	A COWERBOY	BALLAST	BUNGALOW
	ALF PRYCE	CEMENT	CONSERVATORY
	CY BERMAN	SAND	GARAGE
	T BRAKES	STONE	PATH
	VAL HEEGHAM	WOOD	WALL

360 FOURSOME

This couple would like to buy four identical ornaments. Which design will they choose?

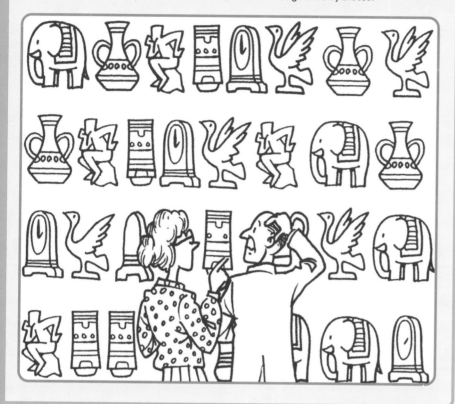

361 CELL STRUCTURE

The object is to create white areas surrounded by black walls, so that:
• Each white area contains only one number
• The number of cells in a white area is equal to the number in it
• The white areas are separated from each other with a black wall
• Cells containing numbers must not be filled in
• The black cells must be linked into a continuous wall
• Black cells cannot form a square of 2 x 2 or larger

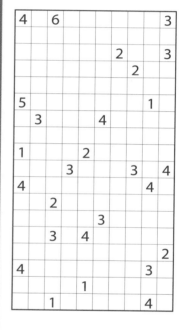

362 SIXTH LETTER

Which of the following five letters logically belongs in the circle marked ?

1) H   2) Z   3) R   4) O   5) J

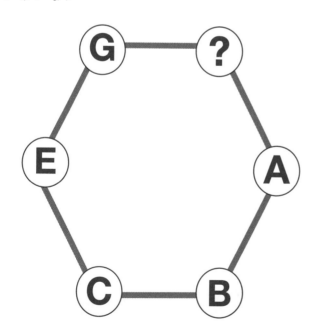

363 IT'S A GIFT

It's that time of year when we should spare a thought for that poor, lovesick male who spent the festive season lugging gifts along to his beloved during the 12 days of Christmas. You'll recollect he dragged a partridge in a pear tree to her house on day one. On day two it was two calling birds and another partridge in another tree. By day twelve the street must have been closed to pedestrians and traffic. The intriguing question is – just how many gifts in total did he foist upon the object of his affections?

364 LOGISTICAL ●●●

Five companies have offices in seven-storey Boreham House, and each has a receptionist in their foyer – which is on the lower floor if they occupy two. From the clues below, can you identify the company occupying each floor or floors, their business, and their receptionist?

Clues

1 The lawyers, whose offices aren't on the fourth floor, don't employ John King.

2 The architects for whom Keith Lyons works have offices higher up the building than those in which Ann Blake is on reception.

3 Gail Hood works for Lorrel & Hardie, whose offices aren't on the seventh floor.

4 Sue Tyler's desk is on a floor two above that of the receptionist who works for publishers Cheape & Chirfle.

5 The fifth and sixth floors of Boreham House are occupied by Kopz & Roberts.

6 Bredd & Cheise aren't the accountants with offices on the third floor.

	Bredd & Cheise	Cheape & Chirfle	Kopz & Roberts	Lorrel & Hardie	Rocke & Rowle	Accountants	Architects	Publishers	Lawyers	Stockbrokers	Ann Blake	Gail Hood	John King	Keith Lyons	Sue Tyler
First/second															
Third															
Fourth															
Fifth/sixth															
Seventh															
Ann Blake															
Gail Hood															
John King															
Keith Lyons															
Sue Tyler															
Accountants															
Architects															
Publishers															
Lawyers															
Stockbrokers															

Record in this grid all the information obtained from the clues, by using a cross to indicate a definite 'no' and a tick to show a definite 'yes'. Transfer these to all sections of the grid thus eliminating all but one possibility, which must be the correct one.

Office floor	Company name	Business	Receptionist

367 DICEY BUSINESS

In order to answer that all-important social question – how many are out to lunch? – four dice are thrown. The answers to the first two throws are given. So what is the answer for the third throw?

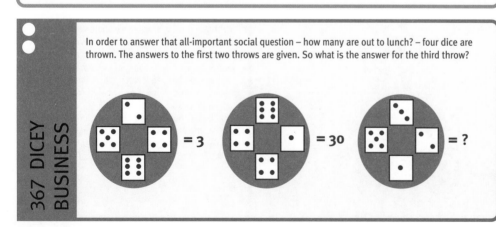

365 SIX-PACK ●●

By packing numbers in the empty spaces, can you make the numbers in each of the 16 hexagons add up to 25? No two numbers in each hexagon may be the same and you can't use zero. We've started you off.

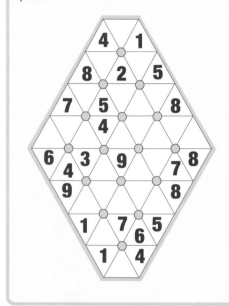

366 NUMBER SQUARES ●●

Can you complete the grid below with the aid of the numbers given, so that all sums, whether horizontal or vertical, are correct? (Please note that each sum should be treated separately.)

48	÷		=		+		=	44
−		+		×		÷		−
	÷	4	=		÷		=	
=		=		=		=		=
	+		=	32	+		=	
×		+		+		+		+
	+		=		+	1	=	
=		=		=		=		=
64	−		=		+		=	53

368 BOARD STIFF

Five firms have handed a directorship to a knight, in order to add that little something to the headed notepaper. Can you complete the details?

1 Sir John Snyfe has joined neither the insurance firm or KGH and R T Fish is chairman of none of these three. A C Maynes is not on the board of KGH which is not the construction company.
2 B N Kew is chairperson of neither the banking firm nor PNT and none of these three has added Sir Jestife to the strength.
3 Neither OBD nor the public relations firm is the one which has taken on Sir Tayne-Lee and LD Rhado chairs none of these three companies.
4 Sir Vance-Hall has joined neither PNT nor the construction company nor is any of these three connected with R T Fish or T D Huss who chairs LTP.
5 A C Maynes does not chair the public relations company or the insurance company which is not the one with L D Rhado on its board and none of these four firms has signed up Sir Fitz-Tension who has not joined the banking firm.

SIR	COMPANY	BUSINESS	CHAIRPERSON
FITZ-TENSION	KGH	BANKING	A C MAYNES
	LTP	CONSTRUCTION	B N KEW
	OBD	INSURANCE	L D RHADO
	PNT	P.R.	R T FISH
	RTC	TRAVEL	T D HUSS
JESTIFE	KGH	BANKING	A C MAYNES
	LTP	CONSTRUCTION	B N KEW
	OBD	INSURANCE	L D RHADO
	PNT	P.R.	R T FISH
	RTC	TRAVEL	T D HUSS
JOHN SNYFE	KGH	BANKING	A C MAYNES
	LTP	CONSTRUCTION	B N KEW
	OBD	INSURANCE	L D RHADO
	PNT	P.R.	R T FISH
	RTC	TRAVEL	T D HUSS
TAYNE-LEE	KGH	BANKING	A C MAYNES
	LTP	CONSTRUCTION	B N KEW
	OBD	INSURANCE	L D RHADO
	PNT	P.R.	R T FISH
	RTC	TRAVEL	T D HUSS
VANCE-HALL	KGH	BANKING	A C MAYNES
	LTP	CONSTRUCTION	B N KEW
	OBD	INSURANCE	L D RHADO
	PNT	P.R.	R T FISH
	RTC	TRAVEL	T D HUSS

369 DARTING ABOUT

A dart player scores 75 with three darts hitting a treble, a double and a single (no bulls). Given that the three numbers that he hits add up to 35 and that the difference between the largest and smallest numbers is 14, can you work out how his score is made up?

Treble	Double	Single

370 TOTALIENS

Each Seasonal Sign has a value in the range 1 to 8 and has the same value wherever it occurs. The numbers around two edges give the total of the values in each row or column. Can you work out the correct value for each symbol which will give these totals?

30	32	27	31	33	30	
						27
						31
						31
						24
						20
						23
						27

371 MIND JOGGER

Can you find five consecutive numbers that add up to 490?

490

372 HOUSE THAT AGAIN

To the untutored eye the houses on the Merryview estate look pretty much alike. Which is why Don, a trainee realtor's tea maker, made plenty of notes on his few excursions.

Clues

1 Houses with double-glazing have central heating.
2 Houses with red roofs have front gardens.
3 Odd numbered houses have green doors.
4 Houses with iron gates have fierce dogs.
5 Houses with green doors have red roofs.
6 Houses with few visitors have white paintwork.
7 Houses without chimneys have leaded windows.
8 Houses with fierce dogs have few visitors.
9 Houses with plastic gnomes have double-glazing.
10 Detached houses have iron gates.
11 Houses with central heating do not have chimneys.
12 Houses with front gardens have plastic gnomes.
13 Even numbered houses are detached.

When asked, by a prospective client, what sort of house number 51 was, the only reply received was an 'umm', an 'agh' and a quick, nervous wipe round the inside of a hot collar. How much of a description can you give from this informative set of notes?

374 ARROW NUMBERS

Each number already in the grid shows the sum of the digits in the line whose direction is shown by the arrow. Only one digit can be placed in each square. There are no zeros. For each sum, each digit can only appear once – e.g., 8 cannot be completed with 44. A sequence of digits forming a sum can only appear once in the grid. If 8 is 53 somewhere then another 8 cannot also be 53. Nor could it be 35, but must contain a different set of digits, such as 71/17, or 62/26. Can you put logic, rather than higher maths, to work and find the unique solution?

373 NUMBERCROSTIC

The two lower grids contain 12 equations, only the answers to which are given. These answers (without altering the order of their digits) also fit randomly into the 12 spaces in the first column of the right-hand grid (to read downwards), and thus form the first digits of the answers to the clues. As you start to fill in the answers, transfer each digit to the corresponding square in the lower grids and begin to piece together the equations.

Clues

A Both digits are the same
B Square of A; reverse of the square of Z
C B – Z
D A x 4
E C – D; palindromic number
F D x 5; two-thirds of C
G First and second digits are 4 times the third digit
H G + A
J F – G – H
K First digit is the square root of the second and third
L J + K; N x 7
M Digits of L rearranged, each in a different position
N G – Z
P M – N
Q Second digit is the sum of the first and third digits
R N + P + Q
S All the digits are the same
T D x 2
U S – T
V Second and third digits are 5 times the first digit
W Descending consecutive odd digits
X Third digit is the sum of the first and second digits
Y B x 6
Z A x 3

A	39	62	
B	5	48	28	64
C	6	43	32	
D	16	41	10	
E	36	67	60	
F	21	53	56	
G	23	30	47	
H	66	27	44	
J	29	51	8	
K	17	57	13	
L	46	63	7	
M	40	11	65	
N	34	42	4	
P	58	12	45	
Q	71	25	54	
R	37	18	3	
S	59	72	38	
T	69	33	26	
U	9	22	50	
V	55	15	52	
W	70	1	35	
X	49	68	14	
Y	61	24	19	2
Z	20	31	

W1	Y2	+	R3	N4	+	B5	C6	=	6	9
L7	J8	+	U9	D10	+	M11	P12	=	9	1
K13	X14	+	V15	D16	–	K17	R18	=	3	8
Y19	Z20	+	F21	U22	–	G23	Y24	=	7	4
Q25	T26	–	H27	B28	+	J29	G30	=	5	6
Z31	C32	–	T33	N34	+	W35	E36	=	4	7
R37	S38	–	A39	M40	–	D41	N42	=	2	2
C43	H44	–	P45	L46	–	G47	B48	=	3	1
X49	U50	+	J51	V52	–	F53	Q54	=	1	3
V55	F56	+	K57	P58	–	S59	E60	=	2	5
Y61	A62	–	L63	B64	+	M65	H66	=	8	6
E67	X68	–	T69	W70	+	Q71	S72	=	6	2

375 IDENTIGRIDS

Can you spot which three squares are identical? Watch out – they may not be the same way up!

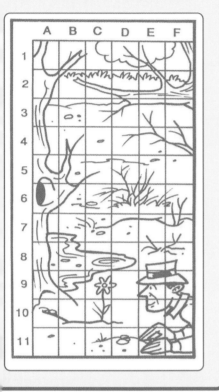

376 SEARCH PARTY

Four of the six shapes at the top are hidden in the main picture. Can you spot which four and whereabouts they are?

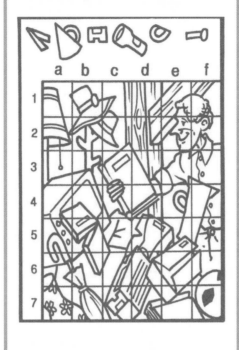

377 DARTING ABOUT

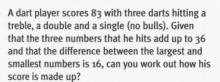

A dart player scores 83 with three darts hitting a treble, a double and a single (no bulls). Given that the three numbers that he hits add up to 36 and that the difference between the largest and smallest numbers is 16, can you work out how his score is made up?

Treble   **Double**   **Single**

378 CAROUSEL

The Carousel is a popular ride with the toddlers at Orles Fair. There are eight different animals on it and so that the children don't get bored with it Sid Slick, the owner, changes the positions of the animals each day. With the position of the horse given and the knowledge that the animals face and move in a clockwise direction, see if you can use the clues to work out the positions of each animal and child on today's ride.

Clues

1 No child is next to or opposite another with the same number of letters in his/her name.
2 Each neighbour has a different number of letters in his/her name.
3 Both mythical animals have boys on them and both birds have girls on them.
4 Bob is opposite the emu and two places behind Chloe, whose neighbours are both boys.
5 The zebra is two places in front of the dragon.
6 Sue is opposite the camel and Alan is opposite the elephant.
7 David is two places in front of the horse but is not next to the emu.
8 There are also a unicorn and a peacock, and the other riders are Edward, Helena and Joan.

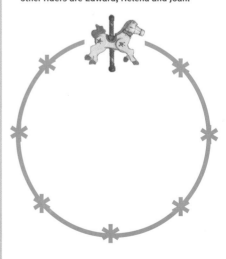

379 SEARCH FOR A RAINBOW

The seven colours of the rainbow (red, orange, yellow, green, blue, indigo, violet) appear just once in the correct order in this grid, running in either a forward or backward direction, either vertically, horizontally or diagonally. Can you locate the rainbow?

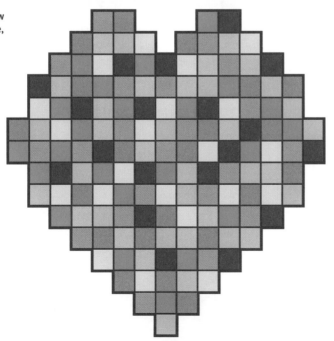

380 MIXED PAIRS

For their annual bowls tournament this year, the Tisbury club has arranged a novel competition. Four married couples, that had fought their way through earlier rounds playing with their spouses, now played three final rounds without them. In each round, nobody played with his/her spouse and each partnered a different member of the opposite gender in each round. After the three rounds, each individual player counted up the points (shots, for the bowls-literate) his/her pair had scored in each round. Each married couple then added their two totals together. The couple with the highest combined total score won the competition. From the facts shown on the master scoreboard, can you name each couple, give their occupations and then name the eventual winners?

	Round 1			Round 2			Round 3	
SHE	SCORE	AND HE	SHE	SCORE	AND HE	SHE	SCORE	AND HE
Caterer's wife	15	Mr Kelly	Thelma	11	Director's husband	Mechanic's wife	17	Teacher's husband
	v			v			v	
Mail lady	10	Butcher	Brenda	8	Sculptor's husband	Director	16	Mr Watson

	Round 1			Round 2			Round 3	
Ann	14	Pete	Clive's wife	12	Jack	Len's wife	14	Clive Dawson
	v			v			v	
Vet's wife	6	Len	Rose	5	Mechanic	Teacher	14	Mr Morris

381 DOT-TO-DOT

Join the dots from 1 to 51 to reveal the hidden picture.

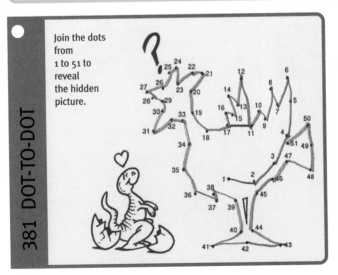

382 NUMBER SQUARES

Can you complete the grid with the aid of the numbers given, so that all sums, whether horizontal or vertical, are correct? (Please note that each sum should be treated separately.)

36	+		=		−		=	22
−		−				−		−
	+		=	25	−		=	
=		=				=		=
	+	7	=		−	9	=	
+		+				+		+
	+		=	26	−		=	
=		=				=		=
31	+		=		−		=	37

383 TRYING TIMES

Substitute each letter with a digit (0–9) so that this long multiplication sum works out correctly.

```
        A B C D
        F E F E   x
      G E D F F
      E H B G E
    G E D F F
    E H B G E
  E A E C J K J F
```

385 IDENTIGRIDS

Which of the three small squares are exactly the same? Watch out, they may not be the same way up!

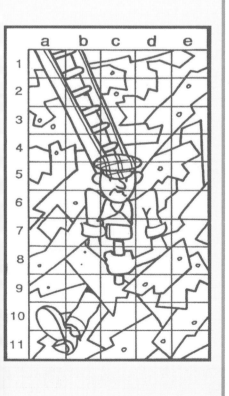

384 FIDDLEHAM APARTMENTS

The super of these notorious apartments continues to confuse visitors with his addiction to Invicta's game Master Mind. Instead of "Smith's in Apartment X, buddy," he hands the visitor a list of current residents and asks him to make guesses as to who is in each apartment. He then marks the line of guesses with two numbers:

First: how many are exactly right – the correct name on the right door.
Second: how many of the names are correct for that floor but are on the wrong door. The only other information he gives is that each surname can only occur on one floor – if Smith is on the ground floor, that name can't be on either of the other two floors. However, the same name can occur more than once on the same floor.
From the 12 guesses below and the list of names on the right, can you work out the correct name for each apartment?

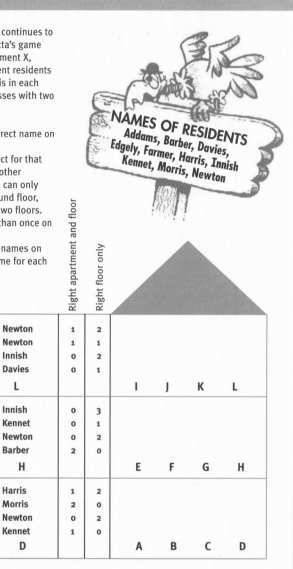

NAMES OF RESIDENTS
Addams, Barber, Davies, Edgely, Farmer, Harris, Innish Kennet, Morris, Newton

					Right apartment and floor	Right floor only					
1	Newton	Harris	Innish	Newton	1	2					
2	Davies	Newton	Davies	Newton	1	1					
3	Kennet	Davies	Edgely	Innish	0	2					
4	Innish	Harris	Barber	Davies	0	1					
	I	J	K	L				I	J	K	L
5	Morris	Barber	Addams	Innish	0	3					
6	Davies	Davies	Farmer	Kennet	0	1					
7	Kennet	Innish	Morris	Newton	0	2					
8	Addams	Farmer	Harris	Barber	2	0					
	E	F	G	H				E	F	G	H
9	Davies	Kennet	Davies	Harris	1	2					
10	Harris	Davies	Barber	Morris	2	0					
11	Farmer	Barber	Harris	Newton	0	2					
12	Addams	Davies	Newton	Kennet	1	0					
	A	B	C	D				A	B	C	D

386 NUMBER SQUARES

Can you complete the grids below with the aid of the numbers given, so that all sums, whether horizontal or vertical, are correct? (Please note that each sum should be treated separately.)

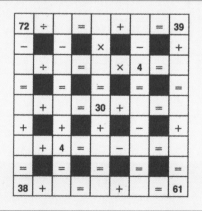

387 MAZE MYSTERY

Travel from the entrance to the exit of the maze, filling the path completely to create a picture.

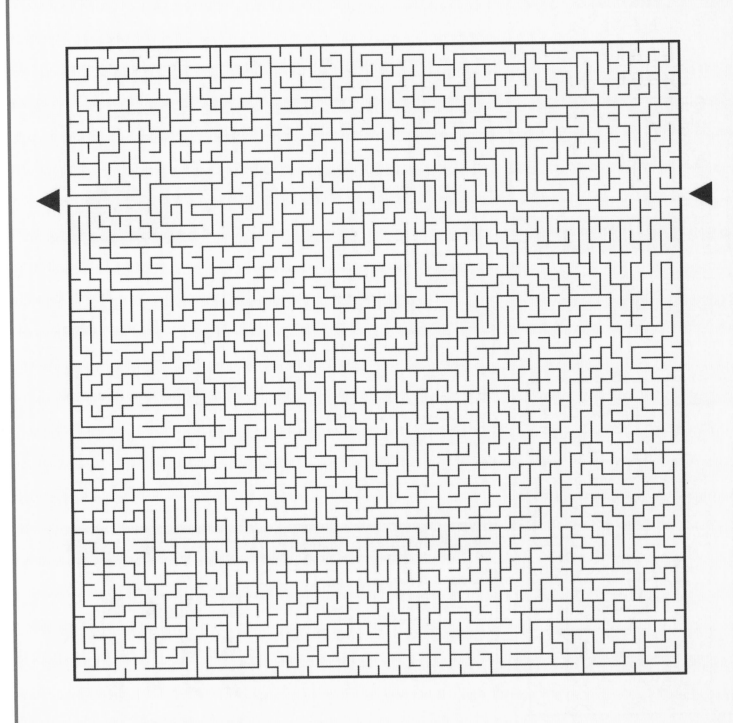

388 WALKIES

Four of the six shapes at the top are hidden in the main picture. Can you spot which four and whereabouts they are?

389 STRESSED MANAGEMENT

Four stressed executives have each taken up with a relaxation system having an oriental flavour. If it is not too much of a strain, can you work out the name of each tense soul, the company each suffers at and the method being tried?

Clues

1 Dee rolls Chinese iron balls in his hand and is known around his office as 'Captain Queeg' but he is not Nathan who works for Just Loans.

2 Poppin can, appropriately, be found looking like a sick hedgehog with acupuncture needles sticking out in all directions. She is not the one with the forename of Ellis.

3 Elsa does not work for J C Nutts and neither of these two is the one who listens to sitar music all day.

4 The employee at U B Loopy does yoga and can be found upside down on her monitor most afternoons. She is not Tewitt. Val Heegham does not work for Hi-Fi Nants.

ACUPUNCTURE

ELLIS	ELSA	FORENAME
NATHAN	VAL	
~~DEE~~	HEEGHAM	SURNAME
POPPIN	TEWITT	
HI-FI NANTS	JC NUTTS	COMPANY
JUST LOANS	U B LOOPY	

CHINESE BALLS

ELLIS	~~ELSA~~	FORENAME
~~NATHAN~~	VAL	
(DEE)	~~HEEGHAM~~	SURNAME
~~POPPIN~~	~~TEWITT~~	
HI-FI NANTS	JC NUTTS	COMPANY
~~JUST LOANS~~	U B LOOPY	

SITAR MUSIC

ELLIS	ELSA	FORENAME
NATHAN	VAL	
~~DEE~~	HEEGHAM	SURNAME
POPPIN	TEWITT	
HI-FI NANTS	JC NUTTS	COMPANY
JUST LOANS	U B LOOPY	

YOGA

ELLIS	ELSA	FORENAME
NATHAN	VAL	
~~DEE~~	HEEGHAM	SURNAME
POPPIN	TEWITT	
HI-FI NANTS	JC NUTTS	COMPANY
JUST LOANS	U B LOOPY	

390 CELL STRUCTURE

The object is to create white areas surrounded by black walls, so that:
- Each white area contains only one number
- The number of cells in a white area is equal to the number in it
- The white areas are separated from each other with a black wall
- Cells containing numbers must not be filled in
- The black cells must be linked into a continuous wall
- Black cells cannot form a square of 2 x 2 or larger

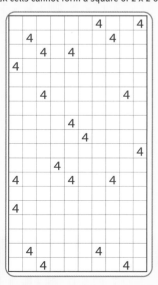

391 THAT LITTLE BIT OF DIFFERENCE

There are eight differences between the two cartoons. Can you spot them?

392 SCATTERPILLAR

Can you reconstruct the six fragments into two identical pillars?

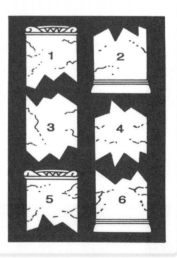

393 HEADLINES

When Pop Star Harry Splitter throws a party the world soon knows about it. Five papers have reported on his latest gathering. In the clues below the papers and headlines are muddled, so that none of the words belong with any of the other three. Can you put the right headlines back into their respective papers?

1. The Daily Standard said Hilarious Romp
2. The Morning Argus said Outrageous Orgy
3. The Daily Chronicle said Hilarious Antics
4. The Evening Chronicle said Mad Party
5. The Weekly Echo said Wild Antics
6. The Sunday News said Outrageous Binge
7. The Daily Argus said Jolly Antics
8. The Sunday Standard said Wild Romp
9. The Weekly News said Jolly Party
10. The Evening News said Outrageous Antics

HINT: What title goes with Antics? So which paper is it in?

PAPER	PAPER	HEADLINE	HEADLINE
	ARGUS	HILARIOUS	ANTICS
	CHRONICLE	JOLLY	BINGE
DAILY	ECHO	MAD	ORGY
	NEWS	OUTRAGEOUS	PARTY
	STANDARD	WILD	ROMP
	ARGUS	HILARIOUS	ANTICS
	CHRONICLE	JOLLY	BINGE
EVENING	ECHO	MAD	ORGY
	NEWS	OUTRAGEOUS	PARTY
	STANDARD	WILD	ROMP
	ARGUS	HILARIOUS	ANTICS
	CHRONICLE	JOLLY	BINGE
MORNING	ECHO	MAD	ORGY
	NEWS	OUTRAGEOUS	PARTY
	STANDARD	WILD	ROMP
	ARGUS	HILARIOUS	ANTICS
	CHRONICLE	JOLLY	BINGE
SUNDAY	ECHO	MAD	ORGY
	NEWS	OUTRAGEOUS	PARTY
	STANDARD	WILD	ROMP
	ARGUS	HILARIOUS	ANTICS
	CHRONICLE	JOLLY	BINGE
WEEKLY	ECHO	MAD	ORGY
	NEWS	OUTRAGEOUS	PARTY
	STANDARD	WILD	ROMP

394 DOT-TO-DOT

Join the dots from 1 to 41 to reveal the hidden picture.

395 IDENTIGRIDS

Which of the three small squares are exactly the same. Watch out, they may not be the same way up.

396 FOURSOME

This man would like to buy four identical vases. Which design will he choose?

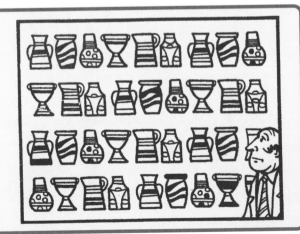

397 TAG GRAPPLERS

Four wrestlers are in the ring ready for a tag wrestling event. The clues are waiting for you to make the introductions.

Clues

1 The Crusader is in purple trunks and Jack the Warrior will take on a Caped opponent.
2 Tom – who calls himself the Secret – is opposing the black-trunked Avenger.
3 Fred's partner is the Masked Gladiator who is not in silver trunks.
   Clue 1 has been entered for you

DON

CAPED	HOODED	TITLE
MASKED	SECRET	
AVENGER	CRUSADER	TITLE
GLADIATOR	~~WARRIOR~~	
BLACK	ORANGE	TRUNKS
PURPLE	SILVER	

FRED

CAPED	HOODED	TITLE
~~MASKED~~	SECRET	
AVENGER	CRUSADER	TITLE
~~GLADIATOR~~	~~WARRIOR~~	
BLACK	ORANGE	TRUNKS
PURPLE	~~SILVER~~	

JACK

~~CAPED~~	HOODED	TITLE
MASKED	SECRET	
~~AVENGER~~	~~CRUSADER~~	TITLE
~~GLADIATOR~~	(WARRIOR)	
BLACK	ORANGE	TRUNKS
~~PURPLE~~	SILVER	

TOM

CAPED	HOODED	TITLE
MASKED	~~SECRET~~	
~~AVENGER~~	CRUSADER	TITLE
GLADIATOR	~~WARRIOR~~	
~~BLACK~~	ORANGE	TRUNKS
PURPLE	SILVER	

398 QUEENS HIGH

If you can rustle up eight counters or coins, or have the strength to make eight crosses, you could use our chessboard to try an old puzzle.

Place the eight counters so that no two are in the same line across or down or diagonally. If you choose, say, A3 then you could not put a mark in any other square in column A or in row 3 nor in squares like C1 and D6 which are in a diagonal line from A3.

The real puzzle, though, is to choose your eight squares, according to the rule, so that the total of the eight numbers you mark is as high as possible. Just how many can you score with your eight queens on each of these chessboards?

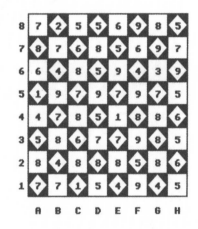

399 QUILTESSENTIAL

In this patchwork quilt, squares of material have been sewn together – each square being either Blue, Green, Lavender or Red. The numbers in the squares tell you how many of that square and its neighbours are of each colour. A square can have up to eight neighbours:

1	2	3
8	x	4
7	6	5

3 0 / 1 0	4 0 / 0 2	1 1 / 0 4	1 4 / 0 1	4 2 / 0 0	4 0 / 0 2		0 1 / 0 3
	4 0 / 4 1	3 1 / 1 4	1 4 / 0 4	4 5 / 0 0	5 2 / 0 2	2 2 / 0 5	
1 0 / 4 1	4 0 / 4 1	2 3 / 1 3	4 3 / 0 2	4 3 / 1 1	2 0 / 3 4		0 3 / 1 2
	0 1 / 5 3	1 3 / 4 1	2 4 / 2 1	6 1 / 1 1	2 1 / 3 3	0 3 / 4 2	
0 3 / 1 2	0 1 / 3 5	0 5 / 3 1	2 2 / 3 2	3 0 / 1 5	0 1 / 6 2		0 4 / 2 0
	0 5 / 0 4	1 3 / 1 4	2 3 / 4 0	1 0 / 4 4	3 0 / 2 4	3 3 / 3 0	
0 4 / 0 2	2 4 / 0 3	4 3 / 0 2	1 3 / 4 1	1 0 / 4 4	5 1 / 2 1		4 2 / 0 0
	1 3 / 0 5	5 2 / 0 2	3 5 / 1 0	0 4 / 4 1	3 1 / 4 1	6 0 / 3 0	
0 1 / 0 3	3 1 / 0 2	3 3 / 0 0	0 5 / 1 0	0 2 / 4 0	2 0 / 4 0		2 0 / 2 0

Sadly, there is no pretty picture – just chunks of colours. Using brain power alone, can you work out the colour of each patch?

400 BALANCING THE SCALES

How many forks are needed to balance scale C?

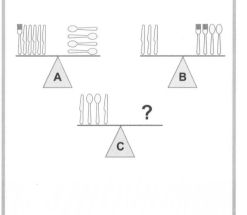

401 DARTING ABOUT

A dart player scores 77 with three darts hitting a treble, a double and a single (no bulls). Given that the three numbers that he hits add up to 41 and that the difference between the largest and smallest numbers is 12, can you work out how his score is made up?

Treble Double Single

402 SHELLING OUT

In an effort to distract the children from playing with an incoming oil slick, Mrs Mumble persuaded them to gather up a pile of relatively clean shells and play a simple game. The two players would take turns to remove one, two, or three shells from the pile and add them to their own store. When all the shells had been taken, the child with the *odd number* of shells would be the winner.

Later, while poring over the holiday snaps, nobody could remember, in this particular game, whose turn it was next. In fact, it doesn't matter! Whoever is next to play, there is a quantity of shells that can be taken, which will ensure that player wins the game. How many is that – one, two or three?

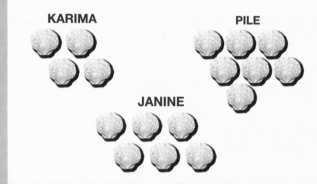

KARIMA   PILE

JANINE

403 CELL STRUCTURE

The object is to create white areas surrounded by black walls, so that:

* Each white area contains only one number.
* The number of cells in a white area is equal to the number in it.
* The white areas are separated from each other with a black wall.
* Cells containing numbers must not be filled in.
* The black cells must be linked into a continuous wall.
* Black cells cannot form a square of 2 x 2 or larger.

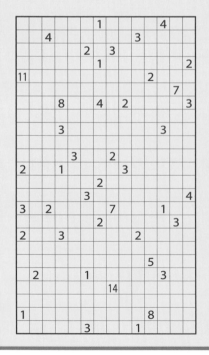

404 SHARP'S SUPERSTORE

When Mr Smith was appointed manager of a brand new Sharp's supermarket, he was faced with the task of stocking the shelves, following guidelines given by the area manager. Can you help Smith sort stock on Sharp's shelves?

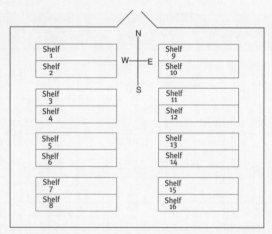

"Don't mix commodities up on the shelves. The cookies and frozen vegetables must face the wall, but put them on opposite sides of the store. Obviously, both fridges should be back to back, with the fruit juices/cordials facing the frozen meat."

"All the non-consumable items including the pet food should be stocked in the same area. I suggest the far south-west corner. The soap powder should be opposite the cleaning fluids and back to back with the pet food."

"All the tinned produce must be on the east side of the store, with the tinned meat and tinned vegetables back to back. Put the tinned fruit on a north-facing shelf and the tinned meat on a south-facing shelf, opposite the home baking produce. The home baking produce should be in the same row as the pet food."

"Cakes and cookies should be back to back, with the candy in the same row as the cakes and facing south."

"Reserve shelf 3 for the tea and coffee and remember to find shelves for the bread and kitchen ware."

405 COACH AND FOUR

Anyone who has tuned into American Football lately will have noticed that more people are directly involved in each pile-up than the overgrown King Kongs on the pitch. Radio links join coach to spy-in-stand; video films are made – and why do you think the Shuttle has been up so often launching all those satellites?

Even at local level, knowing the opposition is everything. Mary's son, Fred, is a player in a four team mini-league. His friend Ed plays for a different team.

The keen coaches have scouted the other teams so well that each coach has a sure technique which will enable his team to defeat one of the others. Which means, in turn, that he knows his team will be defeated by one other team. This leaves one team to play where the outcome is debatable. Four players, one from each team, are involved in the following facts concerning forename, surname, mother and father. (No, there are no tricks using divorces or parentage!)

1 George's team can regularly beat Jim's son's team.
2 Mr Clark's son's team can regularly beat the Davis boy's team.
3 Karl's son's team can regularly beat Nancy's son's team.
4 Mrs Davis's son's team can regularly beat Harry's team.
5 Leonard's son's team can regularly beat Ivan's son's team.
6 Pamela's son's team can regularly beat Ornella's son's team.
7 Jim's son's team can regularly beat Mary's son's team.
8 Harry's team can regularly beat Karl's son's team.
9 Mrs Beacham's son's team can regularly beat Mr Clark's son's team.
10 Mary's son's team can regularly beat Mr Clark's son's team.

As a test of your ability to identify all four players, you are asked to identify the Alston boy's parents.

406 DOT-TO-DOT

Join the dots from 1 to 36 to reveal the hidden picture.

407 TWINNED UP

The little girl would like a top identical to the one she is holding. Which one will she choose?

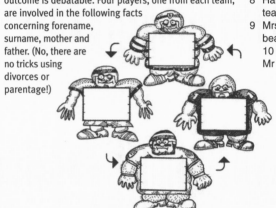

408 ISLAND HOPPING

Each circle containing a number represents an island. The object is to connect each island with vertical or horizontal bridges so that:

* The number of bridges is the same as the number inside the island.
* There can be up to two bridges between two islands.
* Bridges cannot cross islands or other bridges.
* There is a continuous path connecting all the islands.

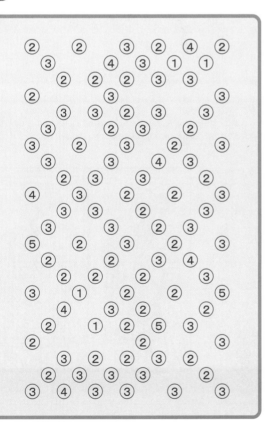

409 QUEENS HIGH

If you can rustle up eight counters or coins, or have the strength to make eight crosses, you could use our chessboard to try an old puzzle. Place the eight counters so that no two are in the same line across or down or diagonally. If you choose, say, A3 then you could not put a mark in any other square in column A or in row 3 nor in squares like C1 and D6 which are in a diagonal line from A3. The real puzzle, though, is to choose your eight squares, according to the rule, so that the total of the eight numbers you mark is as high as possible. Just how many can you score with your eight queens on each of these chessboards?

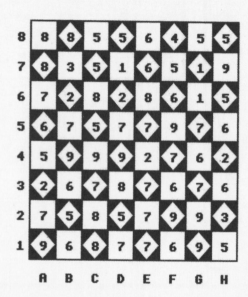

411 BY DEGREES

Four of the six objects lined up at the top are hidden in the picture. Can you see which ones and whereabouts they are?

412 DOT-TO-DOT

Join the dots from 1 to 34 to reveal the hidden picture.

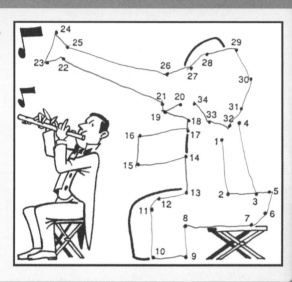

410 POSER

The artist has made five mistakes while trying to paint an exact portrait of the model. Can you spot the five errors?

413 CELL STRUCTURE

The object is to create white areas surrounded by black walls, so that:
* Each white area contains only one number.
* The number of cells in a white area is equal to the number in it.
* The white areas are separated from each other with a black wall.
* Cells containing numbers must not be filled in.
* The black cells must be linked into a continuous wall.
* Black cells cannot form a square of 2 x 2 or larger.

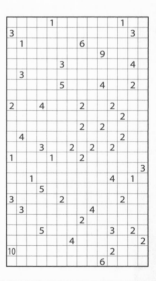

414 IT'S MAGIC

This magic square can be completed using the numbers from 39 to 63 inclusive. To give you a start, looking at the thing as if it was divided into ten columns of digits, we have entered the even digits in the first column, the odd in the second, the even in the third and so on. Can you complete the square so that the five numbers in each row, column and diagonal add up to the magic total? The total – and close your eyes now if you don't want to be told – is 255.

4 5			6 1	4 3
9	4 1	4		7
3	5	6	9	4
4	4	1		6
	6 3	4	4 7	4 9

415 LOGIQUATIONS

In the following problem the digits 0 to 9 are represented by letters. Within each separate puzzle the same letter always represents the same digit. Can you find the correct values each time so that all sums, both horizontal and vertical, are correct? With each separate puzzle, there is a clue to help start you off.

ABC	x	DE	=	CEFC
+		+		–
GHJK	+	DGBB	=	KFGH
BBBG	+	DGKJ	=	KACD

A	B	C	D	E	F	G	H	J	K

Clue: BG + KE = HC

416 DARTING ABOUT

A dart player scores 71 with three darts hitting a treble, a double and a single (no bulls). Given that the three numbers that he hits add up to 35 and that the difference between the largest and smallest numbers is 9, can you work out how his score is made up?

Treble   Double   Single

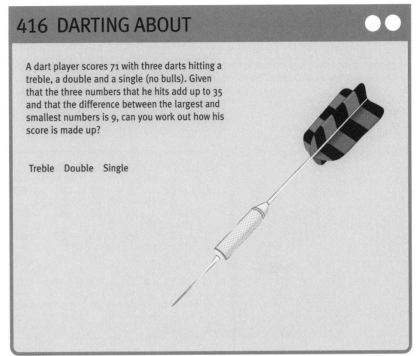

417 LATIN SQUARE

The grid is to be filled with the numbers 1 to 6 so that each number appears exactly once in each row and column. The clues refer to the digit totals in the squares mentioned. For example, DEF2 = 9 would mean that the numbers in D2, E2 and F2 add up to 9.

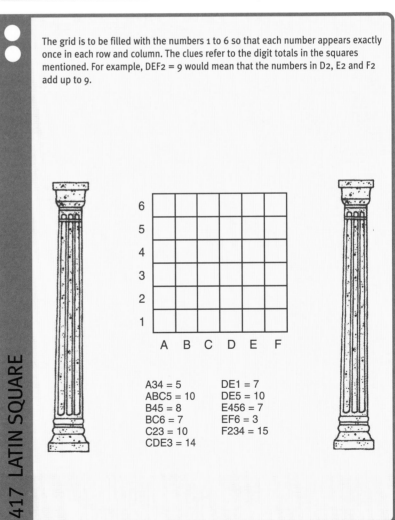

A34 = 5   DE1 = 7
ABC5 = 10   DE5 = 10
B45 = 8   E456 = 7
BC6 = 7   EF6 = 3
C23 = 10   F234 = 15
CDE3 = 14

418 LABYRINTH

Starting at the left hand side, moving forward at each go, try to work your way to the other side. At each step, you must follow the instruction for that column (such as + 4). There are, of course, dead ends. Go on – be amazed!

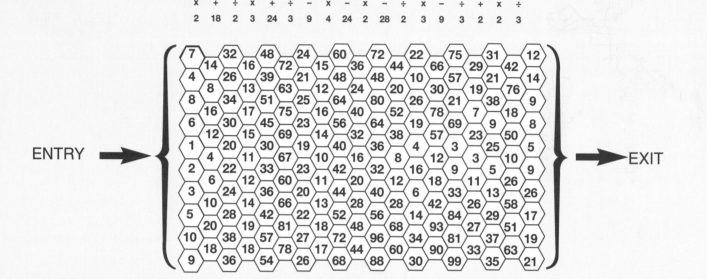

ENTRY → EXIT

419 LATIN SQUARE

Each cell of the square below has one of the digits from 1 to 7. Each row and each column has exactly one of each digit. The clues below give the sum total of the digits in two or more cells. From these clues, can you figure out what number is in each cell?

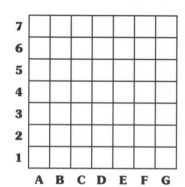

A12=6	C234=16	EFG4=16
ABCD7=10	CD7=5	F23=8
B123=15	DEF6=18	G23=7
B567=12	DEFG3=11	G4567=18
BCD5=18	EFG1=6	

420 CELL STRUCTURE

The object is to create white areas surrounded by black walls, so that:
* Each white area contains only one number.
* The number of cells in a white area is equal to the number in it.
* The white areas are separated from each other with a black wall.
* Cells containing numbers must not be filled in.
* The black cells must be linked into a continuous wall.
* Black cells cannot form a square of 2 x 2 or larger.

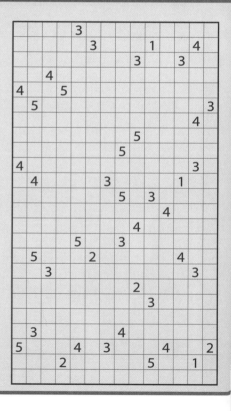

Four of the six objects shown at the top can be found hidden in the picture. Can you see which ones and whereabouts they are?

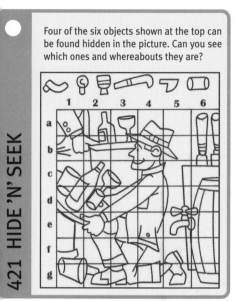

422 TWIN-SET

Two of the pictures shown form a matching pair, while the other two contain one difference each. Can you identify the 'twins' and spot the differences?

423 HIGH FLIERS

Various performers are gathering in London to appear in the Command Performance next week. From the clues given about five of them, can you say on which day they flew into Heathrow, work out the country in which they were previously appearing, and name the airline on which they flew?

Clues

1 Tina Turkey, who did not arrive on a Lo-Cal flight, arrived two days before the Aer Fungus flight from Eire.

2 Sister Sludge arrived on Wednesday, but not from France. The Sabrena flight arrived on Tuesday.

3 Maradonna flew in from the USA two days before the Virgo flight arrived.

4 Englebert Pumpernickel was not the one who arrived on Friday from Germany.

5 Beers For Dears arrived on a Lefthanda flight.

ACT	DAY	COUNTRY	AIRLINE
BEERS FOR DEARS	MONDAY	CANADA	AER FUNGUS
	TUESDAY	EIRE	~~LEFTHANDA~~
	WEDNESDAY	FRANCE	LO-CAL
	THURSDAY	GERMANY	SABRENA
	FRIDAY	USA	VIRGO
ENGELBERT PUMPERNICKEL	MONDAY	CANADA	AER FUNGUS
	TUESDAY	EIRE	LEFTHANDA
	WEDNESDAY	FRANCE	LO-CAL
	THURSDAY	~~GERMANY~~	SABRENA
	~~FRIDAY~~	USA	VIRGO
MARADONNA	MONDAY	CANADA	AER FUNGUS
	TUESDAY	EIRE	LEFTHANDA
	WEDNESDAY	FRANCE	LO-CAL
	THURSDAY	GERMANY	SABRENA
	FRIDAY	~~USA~~	~~VIRGO~~
SISTER SLUDGE	MONDAY	CANADA	AER FUNGUS
	~~TUESDAY~~	EIRE	LEFTHANDA
	~~WEDNESDAY~~	~~FRANCE~~	LO-CAL
	THURSDAY	GERMANY	~~SABRENA~~
	FRIDAY	USA	VIRGO
TINA TURKEY	MONDAY	CANADA	~~AER FUNGUS~~
	TUESDAY	~~EIRE~~	LEFTHANDA
	WEDNESDAY	FRANCE	~~LO-CAL~~
	~~THURSDAY~~	GERMANY	SABRENA
	~~FRIDAY~~	USA	VIRGO

424 BLOOMERS

Charlie Dimwit's garden centre, Bloomers, has a fine display of pot plants for sale. Four gardeners each took ten pots from the stand. Each gardener took a different number of pots of the colours they selected. After they had taken their pots there were an equal number of each colour left over. From the information given can you work out what each gardener selected?

The only colours to be bought by all four gardeners were red and violet and at least two people bought each colour. Rosie bought all colours except blue; she bought one less red than Geoff's greens and two more reds than Ellen's violets. The two ladies bought half the total number of yellow flowers between them. Percy bought all colours except green as did Ellen who bought twice as many blues as Rosie bought yellows. Geoff bought the same number of reds as Percy did violets and together these totalled the same as Rosie's yellows.

425 LATIN SQUARE

Each cell of the square below has one of the digits from 1 to 7. Each row and each column has exactly one of each digit. The clues below give the total of two, three or four cells. From these clues, can you figure out what number is in each cell?

A1234 = 13	D123 = 10
ABC4 = 7	DE3 = 11
ABCD1 = 10	E567 = 6
B567 = 15	EFG2 = 10
BCD6 = 17	EFG5 = 13
C12 = 7	F3456 = 10
CDEF7 = 14	G123 = 11

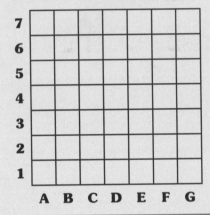

426 SQUARE NUMBERS

The numbers 1 to 25 are arranged randomly in a 5 x 5 square so that no two consecutive numbers are adjacent in any direction or in the same row, column or long diagonal. The corner numbers are all prime; A4 is twice A3; E2 is four times E3, and E4 is twice C4. The single-digit numbers in C2 and D2 appear in the same order reproduced in the number in B1, which is prime; B3 is five times B2. The single-digit number in B5 is ten lower than the number in C5 and six higher than that in B4. D1 is three times D3 but eleven lower than D5. D4 is an odd number. Can you locate each number?

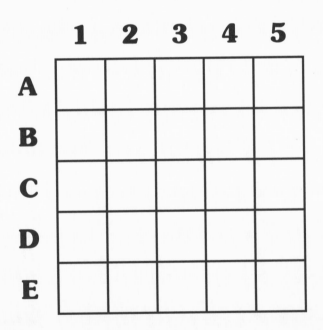

427 WEIGHED UP

How many inkpots are needed to make the third pair of scales balance?

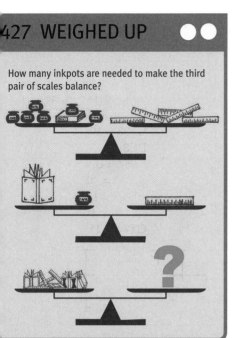

428 LOGIQUATIONS

In the following problem the digits 0 to 9 are represented by letters. Within each separate puzzle the same letter always represents the same digit. Can you find the correct values each time so that all sums, both horizontal and vertical, are correct? With each separate puzzle, there is a clue to help start you off.

ABCD	÷	E	=	EFAF
+		+		+
GHJK	+	CKEF	=	KAEE
FFCH	−	CKGH	=	BGFH

A	B	C	D	E	F	G	H	J	K

Clue: 3 x CD = KF

429 PIECES OF EIGHT

Which pieces (four red and four yellow) can be used to make a square, where all four sides are of equal length? Any piece may be rotated, but not flipped over.

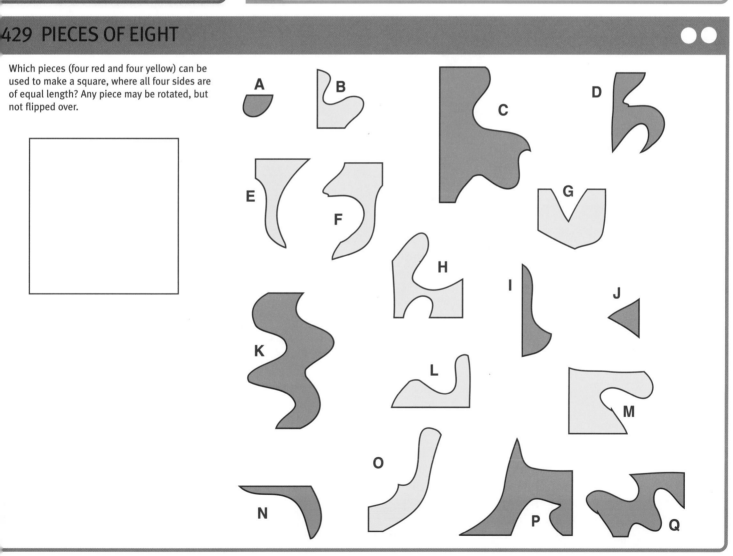

430 WHO WON?

Quite a few race-goers decided to have a drink in the bar and listen to the commentary on the next race through the Tannoy system. Just as the race started, the system went faulty and the commentary was broken up by a series of crackles and whistles. Would you have known from what follows who rode which horse, what number it had and most importantly, *the result?*

"And they're off. Four runners for the *@*@* Chase, Swift Lad, the outsider takes an early lead, *@*@* is second and Willie Parsons on *@*@* third.
@@!?/@@.&!*@@*!**:**@!!?/%**:!@@@**!*@**
Steve Caution on No. 2, *!@*@* now leads, Mother's Joy has taken second place and Crazy Lad is improving –
'@@!?/@@.&!*@@*!**:**'@!!?/%**:!@@@**!*@**
No. 1, *!@* Lad, is running on well and Pat Ellery on *!@*!@* is making a fine challenge.
'@@!?/*@@.&!*@@*!:**'@!!?/**:!@@@**!*@**
Silver Streak is coming up on the rails and is catching Joe Percer on –
'!?/*@@.&!*@@*!**:**'@!!?/%**:!@@@**!*@**

Into the final furlong now and No. *!@*!@*!@*!@* has been pulled up. No. 1, *!@*!@* is leading by a short head from Silver Streak. Willie Parsons is a close third.
'@@!?/@@.&!*@@*!**:**'@!!?/%**:!@@**!*@**
Coming to the line and *!@*!@*!@*!@ wins; No. 2, *!@*!@*!@* the favourite is second and No. 4,*!@* Lad is the last to finish."

432 SILHOUETTE

Shade in every fragment containing a dot – and what have you got?

431 FIDDLEHAM APARTMENTS

The super of these notorious apartments continues to confuse visitors with his addiction to Invicta's game Master Mind. Instead of "Smith's in Apartment X", he hands the visitor a list of current residents and asks him to make guesses as to who is in each apartment. He then marks the line of guesses with two numbers:

First: how many are exactly right with the correct name on the right door?

Second: how many of the names are correct for that floor but are on the wrong door?

The only other information he gives is that each surname can only occur on one floor – if Smith is on the ground floor, that name can't be on either of the other two floors.

However, the same name can occur more than once on the same floor.

From the 12 guesses below and the list of names on the right, can you work out the correct name for each flat?

NAMES OF RESIDENTS
Barber
Carrol
Davies
Farmer
Harris
Jenkin
Quirke
Newton

					Right apartment & floor	Right floor only				
1	Farmer	Carrol	Barber	Barber	2	1				
2	Barber	Jenkin	Harris	Davies	1	1				
3	Newton	Farmer	Barber	Harris	0	1				
4	Newton	Barber	Barber	Harris	0	2				
	I	J	K	L			I	J	K	L
5	Barber	Harris	Harris	Barber	2	0				
6	Harris	Barber	Barber	Quirke	1	1				
7	Quirke	Newton	Farmer	Farmer	0	1				
8	Harris	Newton	Jenkin	Quirke	1	2				
	E	F	G	H			E	F	G	H
9	Barber	Farmer	Newton	Farmer	1	2				
10	Jenkin	Farmer	Jenkin	Farmer	1	1				
11	Newton	Harris	Harris	Newton	2	0				
12	Carrol	Farmer	Carrol	Farmer	1	1				
	A	B	C	D			A	B	C	D

433 FITBITS

Can you identify the two fragments on the left that form part of the main picture?

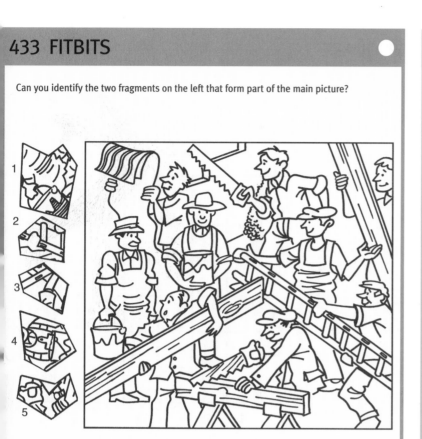

434 POSER

The artist has made five mistakes while trying to paint an exact portrait of the model. Can you spot the five errors?

435 BORDER DISPUTE

Each of these unhappy souls is having trouble with a neighbour. We can't expect you to sort out their problem – doubtless you've enough of your own – but you are invited to discover who is battling with whom, where the warring parties live and the cause of the upset.

Clues

1 The couple at *Justus* are having trouble with the couple at *Wee Kendos*. Those involved are not the Daveys or the Mulveys as these two are, in one way or another, having trouble with the Brewers and the Fletchers neither of whom is responsible for the noise or the slugs.

2 The couple at *Dream Gnome* who are not the Careys or the Daveys are in dispute with the Chaters. The other house involved is not *Wear Ear* where the tree overhangs the neighbouring patio which does not belong to the Daveys.

3 The *Gurneys* at *Our Patch* are the neighbours of neither the Hunters nor the couple at *Pamensam* one of whom is responsible for the slugs flying over the wall and the other for throwing noisy parties.

4 The Fletchers do not live next to *Mortar Pay*. The two with animal problems are the Barneys and the couple living at *Last Stop*. Neither is in dispute with the Packers who live at *The Blotts*.

Name	House	Neighbour	House	Problem

	DREAM GNOME	JUSTUS	LAST STOP	MORTAR PAY	OUR PATCH	BREWER	CHATER	FLETCHER	HUNTER	PACKER	PAMENSAM	SCURGES	THE BLOTTS	WEAR EAR	WEE KENDOS	CATS	FENCE	NOISE	SLUGS	TREE
BARNEY																				
CAREY																				
DAVEY																				
GURNEY																				
MULVEY																				
CATS																				
FENCE																				
NOISE																				
SLUGS																				
TREE																				
PAMENSAM																					
SCURGES																					
THE BLOTTS																					
WEAR EAR																					
WEE KENDOS																					
BREWER																					
CHATER																					
FLETCHER																					
HUNTER																					
PACKER																					

436 SQUARE NUMBERS

The numbers 1–25 are entered randomly in a 5 x 5 square so that there are no two consecutive numbers in any row, column or long diagonal.

The numbers in squares A1 and A4 are prime, the former being two higher than the number in E5. B2 is also prime, and thirteen higher than E1, which is twice D1. D3 is twice D2, which is one lower than B5, which is four higher than C4, which is three times A5. B3 is one higher than C5 but two lower than E3. D5 is twice A4, which is eight lower than C1. A3 is twice D4, and E2 is twice E1. 9 is vertically between 18 and 7, and 6 is one row higher than 8. Can you locate each number?

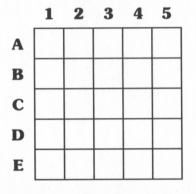

437 LATIN SQUARE

Each cell of the square below has one of the digits from 1 to 7. Each row and each column has exactly one of each digit. The clues below give the total of two, three or four cells. From these clues, can you figure out what number is in each cell?

A567=11   D67=9

ABC2=12   DEFG1=10

AB5=10   DEFG3=22

B456=7   DEF7=6

C123=9   E2345=22

CDE6=15   F456=9

438 BARRELS OF FUN

The 15 barrels in the pub cellar each contain a different whole number of gallons from 6 to 20, none containing the same number as its numerical position counting from the left, and no two consecutive amounts are adjacent. No. 13 contains one gallon more than no. 6, no. 10 one more than no. 1, no. 7 one more than no. 4, no. 14 one more than no. 11, no. 12 one more than no. 9, and no. 3 one more than no. 8. No. 3 contains two more than no. 15, no. 2 two more than no. 9, no. 14 two more than no. 3, and no. 11 two more than no. 8. No. 1 contains three more than no. 2, no. 5 three more than no. 14, no. 7 three more than no. 11, and no. 10 three more than no. 6. If no. 15 does not contain 6 gallons, how much does each contain?

439 SET SQUARE

All the digits from 1 to 9 are used in this grid, but only once each. Can you work out their positions in the grid and make the sums work? We've given two numbers to start you off.

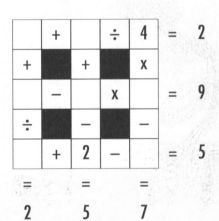

440 SAFE BET

This is a strange safe. Solve all the clues and the combination appears in the shaded squares.

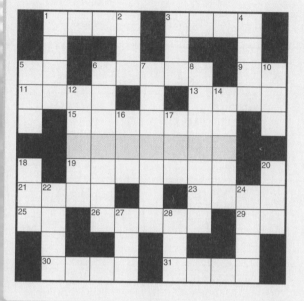

ACROSS

1. Reverse digits of *3 across*
3. Square root of 1,745,041
5. Divide *8 down* by 213,326
6. Multiply *29 across* by *22 down*
9. Divide *10 down* by *29 across*
11. Add 4,875 to *13 across*
13. Multiply *29 across* by 178
15. Cube of *3 down*
19. Cube of *2 down*
21. Multiply *29 across* by 526
23. Subtract *1 down* from *22 down*, then add 10
25. Square root of 7,921
26. 15 per cent of 343,400
29. Cube root of 1,728
30. Multiply *1 down* by 2
31. Add 6,000 to *24 down*

DOWN

1. Multiply *5 across* by 50
2. Half of *5 down*
3. Half of *10 down*
4. Anagram of digits of *3 across*
5. Multiply 16 by 17
6. 25 per cent of 16,486,100
7. Add 3,925,005 to *8 down*
8. Add 144,995 to *6 down*
10. Multiply the last two digits of *24 down* by 8
12. Add 9,809 to *23 across*
14. Square *28 down*
16. Next in series 614, 713, 812,...
17. Add 73 to *16 down*
18. Add *2 down* to *3 down*
20. Add *27 down* to *9 across*
22. Square root of 15,225,604
24. Square root of 1,283,689
27. Multiply *5 across* by 5
28. Divide 1,644 by *29 across*

441 SILHOUETTE

Shade in every fragment containing a dot – and what have you got?

442 TWINNED UP

The twins would like to buy identical vases. Which two will they choose?

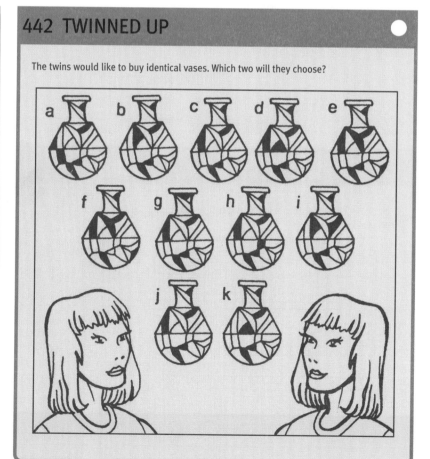

443 LIGHT WORK ●●●

After summer lightning caused havoc in Cable Street, five residents each had to call in an electrical firm and have work done before power could safely be restored. Can you sort out positive from negative and bring a summary to earth?

Clues

1 New lights were needed at the house numbered three higher than the one to which LiveWires were called. Neither of these is the house where A C Maynes lives.

2 Eartha Green lives at No. 6 – she did not need rewiring nor did she call in Glowball Services who replaced a fusebox.

3 Lottie Watts called in Pluggins. Bill Quarterley's house number is four higher than Phil O'Ment's.

4 The wiring was replaced by ShocksRus and the new main installed by Just Sparks. Neither firm visited No. 4.

Hint: Which firm replaced the lights – and at which house?

RESIDENT	NO.	FIRM	PROBLEM
A C MAYNES	3	GLOWBALL SVCS	FUSEBOX
	4	JUST SPARKS	LIGHTS
	6	LIVEWIRES	NEW RING MAIN
	7	PLUGGINS	REWIRING
	10	SHOCKSRUS	SOCKETS
BILL QUARTERLEY	3	GLOWBALL SVCS	FUSEBOX
	4	JUST SPARKS	LIGHTS
	6	LIVEWIRES	NEW RING MAIN
	7	PLUGGINS	REWIRING
	10	SHOCKSRUS	SOCKETS
EARTHA GREEN	3	GLOWBALL SVCS	FUSEBOX
	4	JUST SPARKS	LIGHTS
	6	LIVEWIRES	NEW RING MAIN
	7	PLUGGINS	REWIRING
	10	SHOCKSRUS	SOCKETS
LOTTIE WATTS	3	GLOWBALL SVCS	FUSEBOX
	4	JUST SPARKS	LIGHTS
	6	LIVEWIRES	NEW RING MAIN
	7	PLUGGINS	REWIRING
	10	SHOCKSRUS	SOCKETS
PHIL O'MENT	3	GLOWBALL SVCS	FUSEBOX
	4	JUST SPARKS	LIGHTS
	6	LIVEWIRES	NEW RING MAIN
	7	PLUGGINS	REWIRING
	10	SHOCKSRUS	SOCKETS

444 WIRED UP ●

Which of the four plugs should be inserted in the socket to operate the shaver?

445 CELL STRUCTURE ●●

The object is to create white areas surrounded by black walls, so that:
* Each white area contains only one number.
* The number of cells in a white area is equal to the number in it.
* The white areas are separated from each other with a black wall.
* Cells containing numbers must not be filled in
* The black cells must be linked into a continuous wall.
* Black cells cannot form a square of 2 x 2 or larger.

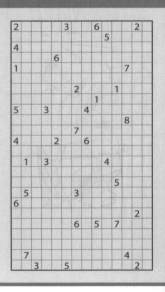

446 GARDENER'S WORLD

The large picture has been reproduced underneath in twelve pieces. However, three of the pieces contain an extra detail, while four pieces have a detail missing. Can you spot all the extra and missing details?

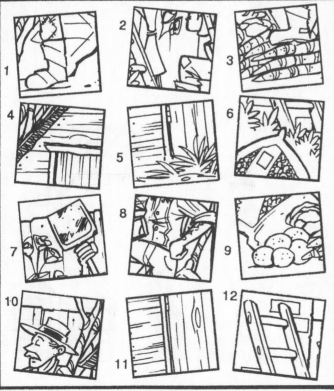

447 PICNIC PARTY

Four happy couples are out for a picnic on Whistleberry Hill. See if you can manage to pair up husband and wife before the rain comes.

448 DROP OUT

The man is choosing a jar. In the bottom picture, he has taken his chosen jar away. Which one?

449 CRIME SQUAD

The criminals involved in the four scenes on the left below were soon arrested by a smart detective who spotted them in the larger picture. Can you spot them as well?

450 LOGIQUATIONS

In the following problem the digits 0 to 9 are represented by letters. Within each separate puzzle the same letter always represents the same digit. Can you find the correct values each time so that all sums, both horizontal and vertical, are correct? With each separate puzzle, there is a clue to help start you off.

AB	x	CDE	=	FCBB
x		+		–
GHJ	+	GDBB	=	GABA
BFKA	+	GCKD	=	EGDA

A	B	C	D	E	F	G	H	J	K

Clue: GH is a prime number

451 LATIN SQUARE

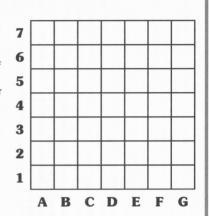

Each cell of the square below has one of the digits from 1 to 7. Each row and each column has exactly one of each digit. The clues below give the total of two, three or four cells. From these clues, can you figure out what number is in each cell?

ABC4=6 DE7=3
B2345=10 E1234=13
BCD1=16 F456=11
BCD6=9 FG2=5
CDE3=10 FG4=12
D567=9 G3456=13

452 ARROW NUMBERS

Each number already in the grid shows the sum of the digits in the line whose direction is shown by the arrow. Only one digit can be placed in each square. There are no zeros. For each sum, each digit can only appear once – e.g., 8 cannot be completed with 44. A sequence of digits forming a sum can only appear once in the grid. If 8 is 53 somewhere then another 8 cannot also be 53. Nor could it be 35, but must contain a different set of digits, such as 71/17, or 62/26. Can you put logic, rather than higher maths, to work and find the unique solution?

	14	29	23	16		25	4	11
26 ▶					10	▶		
					14			
43 ▶			4					
11	▶			8 ▶			11	8
30 ▶		8			10 ▶			
12 ▶					24 ▶	9		

453 TENTACKLE

Eight children are camping, two to each tent, and some have given us a couple of clues as to how to find them. The trouble is their directions are as bad as their cooking and in each case only one direction is true whilst the other is an exact opposite, so that East should read West etc. Directions are not necessarily exact so North could be North, Northeast or Northwest. To help you one child is already tucked into a sleeping bag.

Alice says: "I'm North of Fiona and West of Beth."
Carol says: "I'm South of Helen and East of Gina."
Fiona says: "I'm North of Gina and East of Carol."
Helen says: "I'm South of Daisy and West of Enid."

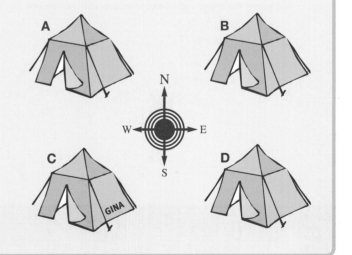

454 FIND THE FAKES

The proud owners of the famous artist's paintings (shown at the top) are showing off their new acquisitions (shown below). Unfortunately, however, five of these are not the artist's original work, but are clever fakes. Which are the five fakes and how can you identify them?

455 TAKE FIVE

Can you break this clock face into *five* pieces so that adding together the numbers on each piece will produce these five totals?

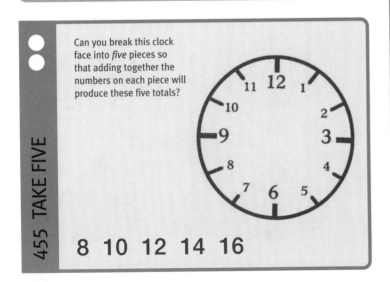

8 10 12 14 16

456 PRIZE DRAW

As usual, there was a prize draw held as part of the local fair and this year all the major prizes went to local people. From the clues below, can you say in what order the prizes were drawn, which were the winning tickets and who bought them?

Clues

1 The second prize drawn, which was the six bottles of home-made wine, went to one of the men.

2 Ticket 161 won the prize which was awarded just before the camera.

3 Ticket 198 won the bicycle; it was not sold to Mrs Smart, who did not hold the highest-numbered ticket.

4 Father Murphy's ticket was number 242.

5 The fifth prize to be drawn went to Mr White.

6 The hair drier went to Mr Copper, whose ticket was drawn just after Mrs Evans'.

	Bicycle	Camera	Food hamper	Hair drier	Wine	161	198	242	504	625	Father Murphy	Mrs Smart	Mr White	Mrs Evans	Mr Copper
First															
Second															
Third															
Fourth															
Fifth															
Father Murphy															
Mrs Smart															
Mr White															
Mrs Evans															
Mr Copper															
161															
198															
242															
504															
625															

Record in this grid all the information obtained from the clues, by using a cross to indicate a definite 'no' and a tick to show a definite 'yes'. Transfer these to all sections of the grid thus eliminating all but one possibility, which must be the correct one.

Order	Prizes	Ticket numbers	Ticket holders

457 TREASURE HUNT

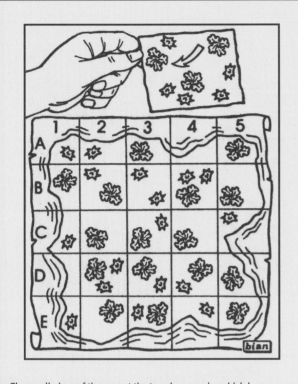

The small piece of the map at the top shows under which large bush the treasure is buried. Can you work out in which square this is in the larger map?

458 SILHOUETTE

Match the picture of gardening tools with its silhouette.

459 LABYRINTH

● ● ●

Starting at the left hand side, moving forward at each go, try to work your way to the other side. At each step, you must follow the instruction for that column (such as x 4). There are, of course, dead ends. Go on – be amazed!

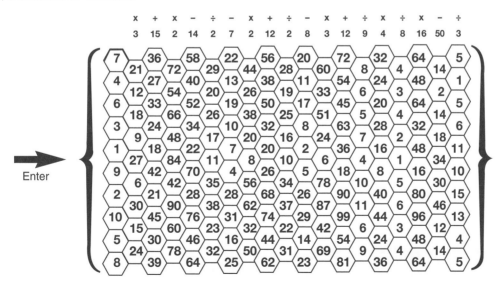

460 IDENTICAL TWINS

Two of these go-karters are identical. Which two?

461 ARROW NUMBERS ●●●

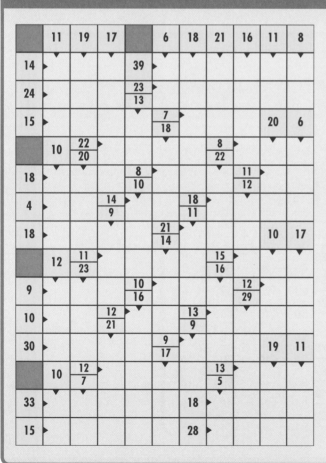

Each number already in the grid shows the sum of the digits in the line whose direction is shown by the arrow. Only one digit can be placed in each square. There are no zeros. For each sum, each digit can only appear once – e.g., 8 cannot be completed with 44. A sequence of digits forming a sum can only appear once in the grid. If 8 is 53 somewhere then another 8 cannot also be 53. Nor could it be 35, but must contain a different set of digits, such as 71/17, or 62/26. Can you put logic, rather than higher maths, to work and find the unique solution?

462 ARROW PUZZLE

Can you help the ship reach America by following the arrows, being careful not to land on Australia by mistake?

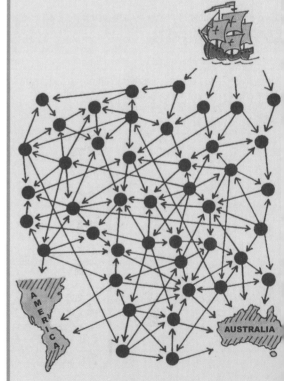

463 TOOL BAG

Four of the six shapes shown at the top can be found hidden in the picture. Which ones and whereabouts are they?

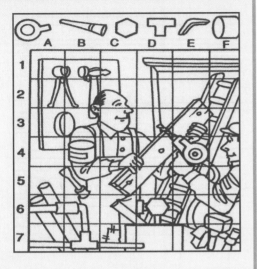

464 FOURSOME

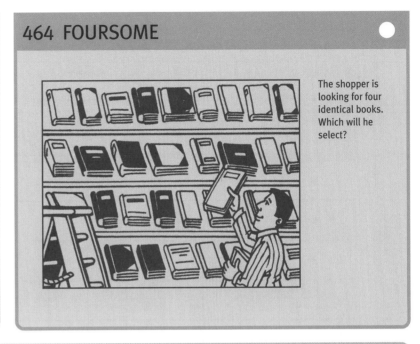

The shopper is looking for four identical books. Which will he select?

465 BLACK OUT

Which three creatures are shown in silhouette at the top?

466 WHO'S WHO?

The five top models parade down the catwalk in turn. Amy, who is immediately in front of Bridget and immediately behind Claudia, is wearing a short skirt and the same belt as Deborah; Elaine is modelling a long skirt. Name the numbers!

467 ARROW NUMBERS

Each number already in the grid shows the sum of the digits in the line whose direction is shown by the arrow. Only one digit can be placed in each square. There are no zeros. For each sum, each digit can only appear once – e.g., 8 cannot be completed with 44. A sequence of digits forming a sum can only appear once in the grid. If 8 is 53 somewhere then another 8 cannot also be 53. Nor could it be 35, but must contain a different set of digits, such as 71/17, or 62/26. Can you put logic, rather than higher maths, to work and find the unique solution?

	10	28	22		19	7	22		28	27
17 ▶				9 ▼				12 ▼		
								9		
21 ▶			37 ▶							
			12 ▼							
26 ▶					25 ▶				
12 ▶			11 ▶		14 ▶				

468 ARROW NUMBERS

Each number already in the grid shows the sum of the digits in the line whose direction is shown by the arrow. Only one digit can be placed in each square. There are no zeros. For each sum, each digit can only appear once – e.g., 8 cannot be completed with 44. A sequence of digits forming a sum can only appear once in the grid. If 8 is 53 somewhere then another 8 cannot also be 53. Nor could it be 35, but must contain a different set of digits, such as 71/17, or 62/26. Can you put logic, rather than higher maths, to work and find the unique solution?

	19	35	13		19	11		37	8	13
7				15			20/11			
21			24/15							
15			10/10			20/20				
	10/9				12/9				6	11
27						9				
13			22				21			

469 MISGIVINGS

Of the six objects shown at the top, four are to be found hidden in the main picture. Which ones, and where are they?

470 LATIN SQUARE

Each cell of the square below has one of the digits from 1 to 7. Each row and each column has exactly one of each digit. The clues below give the total of two, three or four cells. From these clues, can you figure out what number is in each cell?

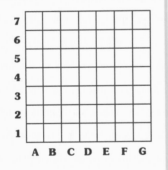

A567=9	CDE3=18	DEFG5=21
AB4=9	CDE7=6	E1234=13
ABCD2=21	D4567=12	F234=7
C234=18	DE4=3	G123=9
C567=7	DEF1=14	

471 LOGIQUATIONS

In the following problem the digits 0 to 9 are represented by letters. Within each separate puzzle the same letter always represents the same digit. Can you find the correct values each time so that all sums, both horizontal and vertical, are correct? With each separate puzzle, there is a clue to help start you off.

ABC	+	DEF	=	GBFH
+		–		+
JDGH	–	GCK	=	JGJE
DBJJ	+	GFA	=	DGCK

Clue: DF is a square

A	B	C	D	E	F	G	H	J	K

472 TOTTERING TOWER

These piles of bricks aren't the random results of child's play – but clues to the final, at present, blank tower on the right. Like the rest, that tower has one brick with each of the six letters. The numbers below each heap tell you two things:
(a) How many adjacent pairs of bricks are actually correct in the final tower.
(b) How many adjacent pairs of bricks make a correct pair but the wrong way up.

So: would score one on the first number if the final tower had an A directly above a C. It would score one on the second number if the final tower had C on top of A. From all of this, can you create the tower before it finally topples?

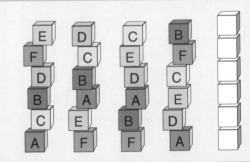

PAIRS					
Correct	0	1	0	1	5
Reversed	2	0	0	0	0

473 URNS-INGS

Which three urns are identical?

474 FIX THE PIC

Basher has broken all the Easter eggs. Can you put them back together again?

475 ARROW NUMBERS

Each number already in the grid shows the sum of the digits in the line whose direction is shown by the arrow. Only one digit can be placed in each square. There are no zeros. For each sum, each digit can only appear once – e.g., 8 cannot be completed with 44. A sequence of digits forming a sum can only appear once in the grid. If 8 is 53 somewhere then another 8 cannot also be 53. Nor could it be 35, but must contain a different set of digits, such as 71/17, or 62/26. Can you put logic, rather than higher maths, to work and find the unique solution?

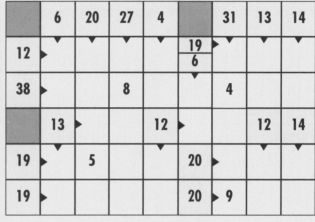

476 SQUARES

The six squares seen highlighted at the top right-hand corner of the grid are repeated in only one other place. Can you see where?

477 SPOT THE DIFFERENCE

Can you spot the eight differences between the two drawings?

478 WEB BROWSING

The spiders are identical, but only three have spun precisely the same web – which three?

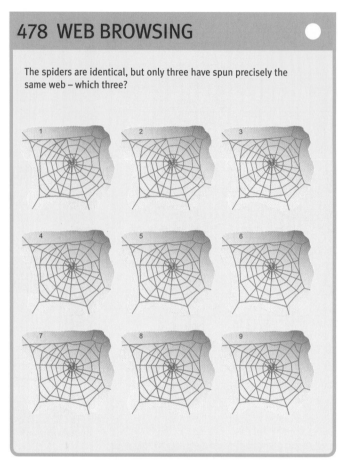

479 ICELANDS

Our walrus has completely gone to pieces! Can you put him back together again?

480 ARROW NUMBERS

Each number already in the grid shows the sum of the digits in the line whose direction is shown by the arrow. Only one digit can be placed in each square. There are no zeros. For each sum, each digit can only appear once – e.g., 8 cannot be completed with 44. A sequence of digits forming a sum can only appear once in the grid. If 8 is 53 somewhere then another 8 cannot also be 53. Nor could it be 35, but must contain a different set of digits, such as 71/17, or 62/26. Can you put logic, rather than higher maths, to work and find the unique solution?

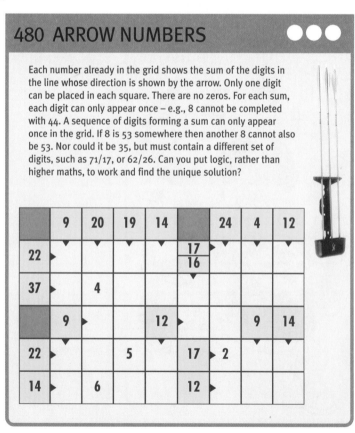

481 NUMBER SEARCH

The number 31425 appears just once in this grid, running in either a forward or backward direction, either verically, horizontally or diagonally. Can you locate it?

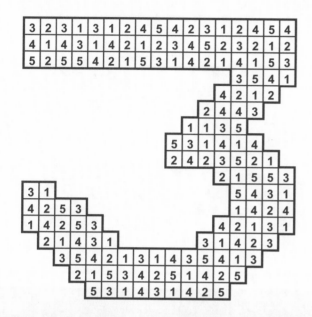

482 TAKE ONE

Remove just one letter and leave all 26 letters of the alphabet...

X	J	N	D	O
K	G	W	P	L
S	C	Q	V	H
R	B	Z	F	T
E	Y	M	U	I	A

484 LATIN SQUARE

Each cell of the square below has one of the digits from 1 to 7. Each row and each column has exactly one of each digit. The clues below give the total of two, three or four cells. From these clues, can you figure out what number is in each cell?

A1234=14
AB1=12
B456=8
BCD3=15
C123=13
C67=9
CDE5=10
D456=18

DEFG2=17
DEFG7=10
E567=7
EFG4=15
F345=12
FG1=5
G567=13

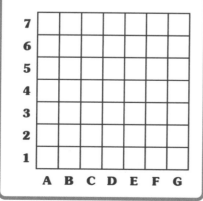

483 CELL STRUCTURE

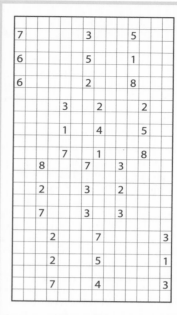

The object is to create white areas surrounded by black walls, so that:
* Each white area contains only one number
* The number of cells in a white area is equal to the number in it
* The white areas are separated from each other with a black wall
* Cells containing numbers must not be filled in
* The black cells must be linked into a continuous wall
* Black cells cannot form a square of 2x2 or larger

485 PIECES OF EIGHT

Which pieces (four red and four yellow) can be used to make a square, where all four sides are of equal length? Any piece may be rotated, but not flipped over.

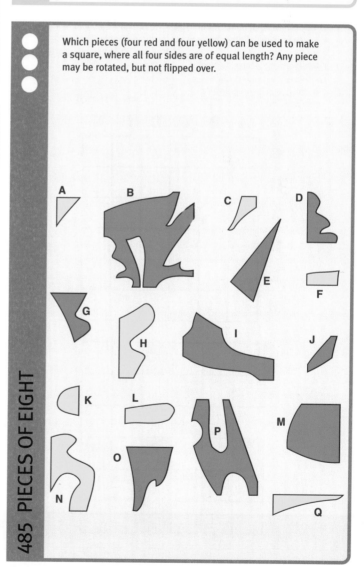

486 2 x 6 x 6

All the clues lead to single or two-digit answers to be filled into the main grid. You must also complete the crossword grid which will help you complete the main grid. Where there are two single-digit answers, they are not adjacent in that row or column. The clues are in no particular order for the indicated row or column. The digit zero only appears in the main grid. Good luck!

COLUMN

A Square root of *2 down*; first two digits of *1 across*; *9 across*, which is twice *11 down*; one less than the other single digit

B Two-digit cube number; two consecutive digits multiplied together; *11 down*, which is a prime number; all digits are different

C Half of *12 across*; half of *14 across*; two more than *5 across*; all digits are different

D Half of *12 across*; first digit is three times the second; five times the first two digits of column A

E (*3 across* reversed) minus one; *6 down*; total of the other two answers

F One-eighth of *7 across*; two consecutive ascending digits; *8 down*, which is three times a prime number

ROW

G Three times *3 across*; square root of *1 across*; two single digits which are consecutive numbers

H Half of *4 down*; quarter of *1 down*; two single digits which total 5

J Cube number, which is also one-quarter of *7 across*; prime number, which is two more than *11 down*; cube number

K *8 down* plus *13 down*, which is also two consecutive numbers multiplied together; three times a cube number; two consecutive numbers multiplied together

L Half a square number; *6 down*; square number

M *15 across*; four times *15 across*; *5 across*

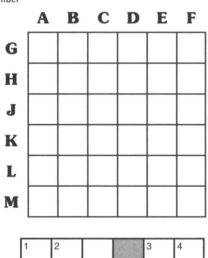

A B C D E F
G
H
J
K
L
M

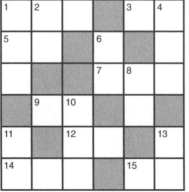

487 STONED

"Here, Harry. Can you place these four stones so that every one is the same distance from the other three?"

"Dunno, Bert. I'll try."

"You'll have a bit of a job on the patio – but you can do it in the garden." How?

488 DOMINO DEAL

A standard set (0 – 0) to (6 – 6) is laid out below. Each domino is placed so that the larger number will be on the bottom:

ie,   3   not   6
      6   3

Those top numbers show the four numbers which form the top half of each domino in that column. The bottom numbers, below the grid, give the four bottom numbers for that column. The seven numbers on the left show the numbers which belong in that row. Can you cross-reference the facts and deduce where each domino had been placed? 1*2 is given as a start.

'TOP' NUMBERS

		01	00	03	01	02	12	0
		35	12	36	22	34	45	14
0 1 1 1 2 3 4								1
0 1 1 2 6 6 6								2
0 0 1 1 2 3 5								
2 3 3 4 4 4 6								
0 0 1 2 3 4 6								
3 4 4 5 5 5 6								
0 0 2 2 3 4 5								
1 3 5 5 5 6 6								
		25	04	34	13	34	25	1
		56	56	66	46	56	56	34

'BOTTOM' NUMBERS

489 OFF FORM

Which one of the eight numbered pieces is the one which is missing from the broken bench?

490 WRAPPED UP

Which of the four numbered cubes is identical to the one held by the boy?

491 POT LUCK

Which of the numbered pots should logically occupy the empty square?

492 WHATEVER NEXT?

Can you give the next letter in this sequence?

A D O P Q ?

493 PILE UP

These piles of bricks aren't the random results of child's play – but clues to the final, at present, blank tower on the right. Like the rest, that tower has one brick with each of the six letters.

The numbers below each heap tell you two things:
(a) How many adjacent pairs of bricks are actually correct in the final tower.
(b) How many adjacent pairs of bricks make a correct pair but the wrong way up.

So:

would score one on the first number if the final tower had an A directly above a C. It would score one in the second number if the final tower had C on top of A. From all of this, can you create the tower before it finally topples?

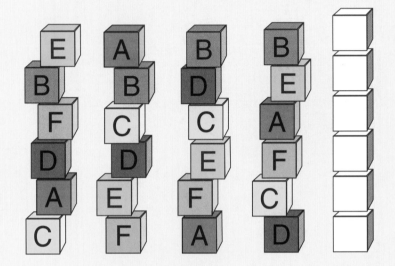

PAIRS					
Correct	0	0	0	0	5
Reversed	0	1	2	2	0

494 CROSS NUMBERWORD

This puzzle uses the device of expressing a three-letter word as a number. This is done by replacing each letter with the number which is its position in the alphabet, A=1, Z=26 so DOG=4157 and PUT=162120. When transposing the numbers back into letters to make a three-letter word, there may be more than one possibility e.g. 22114 could be BUN (2, 21,14) or VAN (22,1,14)

The aim of the puzzle is to complete the crossword grid with three-letter words. You will need to look at the numerical clues to find the numbers to translate into letters for the words in the grid, but you will also need to keep switching to the grid and to any completed words to eliminate impossibilities.

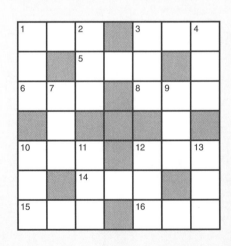

ACROSS
1 Digit total is 17
3 Multiple of 6; can be expressed as three letters in two ways
5 45 times a number which is less than 500
6 75 times a number which is greater than 2,500
8 Less than 1000; digit total is 10
10 Ignoring the first digit, a multiple of 14
12 Four digits
14 Four digits; five times a cube number
15 Less than 14 across; digit total is 19
16 Less than 12 across

DOWN
1 Six digits; 40 times a number which is less than 4000

2 75 times a number which is less than 500; it can be expressed as three letters in three ways
3 Four digits; multiple of 24; letters are in reverse alphabetical order
4 Greater than 2000
7 15 times a number which is greater than 1100; digit total is 21
9 Four digits; not a multiple of 25; 15 times a number which is less than 80
10 Six digits; letters in alphabetical order
11 Less than 14 across
12 Multiple of five; digit total is 17
13 Digit total is 20; five times a number which is greater than 50,000

495 25 OF THE BEST

Twenty-five of the numbers between 1 and 49 have been inserted in the grid. Clues to each of the answers in each row and column are given below, but I must add that the numbers in the long diagonal from top left to bottom right total 112, and the other long diagonal from top right to bottom left totals 137. No two consecutive numbers are in the same row, column or diagonal. Using this information can you complete the original grid?

ACROSS
F D equals twice E; D plus E equals twice A; B equals C plus 9
G C plus E equals B plus D; total equals 116
H B plus D equals E; only one odd number
J A equals seven times C; E equals twice C
K D equals three times B

COLUMN
A G equals twice H
B F plus K equals H plus J; total equals 123
C F plus G equals J plus K; K is a cube number; total equals 84
D K equals twice (F plus H); J is the second highest number
E H equals three times F

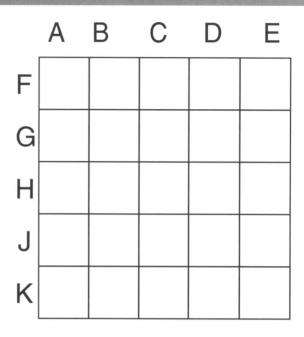

496 NUMBERS UP

Can you discover the logical sequence shown here and work out what number should replace the question-mark?

497 AMAZING

Can you work your way from the entrance at the top to the exit at the bottom of this maze?

498 BLACK OUT

Can you see which two dinosaurs are shown in silhouette at the top?

499 WALKIES

Each picture is missing a detail that is present in the other seven. Can you spot all eight missing details?

500 ON THE LINE

Seven travellers using a provincial city's underground railway alighted at successive stations on their journey from west to east. From the clues given below, can you name each of the stations numbered 1 to 7 (interchange stations being denoted by a circle), and name the passenger who got out there?

Clues

1 Libby had already left the train by the time Nigel got out at King's Grove, which is not an interchange station, though the station where Tessa alighted is.

2 Howard got off the train two stations before Peel Park.

3 Station 3 on the plan is Maple Street.

4 It was a woman who alighted at station 5.

5 Eileen got out at the station before Red Lion.

6 Bradley left the train at station 6, which is further east than Market Cross.

7 One of the men got out at Museum station, which is not numbered 7 on the plan.

Stations: Central Station; King's Grove; Maple Street; Market Cross; Museum; Peel Park; Red Lion

Travellers: Bradley; Conrad; Eileen; Howard; Libby; Nigel; Tessa

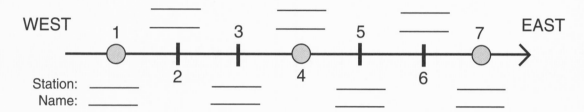

Starting tip: Begin by working out the number indicating King's Grove station.

501 THANKS FOR THE MEMORY

On top of her bookcase Alice has six photographs taken on some of her favourite holidays over the years. From the clues given below, can you indicate in the spaces provided the location and date of each of the photographs lettered A to F in the diagram?

Clues

1 None of the photographs is in its correct chronological position, reading from left to right.

2 The snapshot taken on Lake Garda is next left to the souvenir of Alice's 1959 holiday, while the scene from Cornwall is next right to the picture taken in 1963.

3 The Isle of Man photograph, whose date is earlier than that of the one in position C, is next but one right from the 1975 one.

4 The photo in position E was taken next after the one marked C, while the one bringing back memories of Tenby dates from a later holiday than the one on which photo A, which does not depict a scene from Brittany, was taken.

5 The picture labelled D was taken in the same decade as the one in position B, but in an earlier year.

Location: Assisi; Brittany; Isle of Man; Lake Garda; Tenby
Year: 1959; 1963; 1971; 1972; 1975; 1979

Starting tip: Begin by working out the position of the photo taken in 1959.

502 SUDOKU

	5	1	9		8	3	6	
3	6		4		1		2	8
4			3					5
1	4						7	9
		5			1			
9	8						5	6
6			9					7
5	9		7		6		3	1
	3	7	5		4	6	9	

503 SUDOKU

6	8	3				5	7	9
	4	7		9		3	2	
	1	9	2	3	8	6	4	
7			4		6			1
	6	8	9	7	1	2	5	
	5	1		8		7	9	
2	9	6				4	3	8

504 SUDOKU

		3	2	9	6	1		
			3		1			
8			5	7	4			6
3	8	9				2	6	5
5		6				7		4
7	4	2				9	3	1
2			4	5	9			7
			7		8			
		4	6	1	3	8		

505 SUDOKU

	6		8		3		4	
2		3	5		1	6		8
	4	7				3	1	
5	1			9			3	6
			3		5			
4	3			6			5	7
	5	2				7	9	
9		4	7		6	5		1
	7		9		2		6	

506 SUDOKU

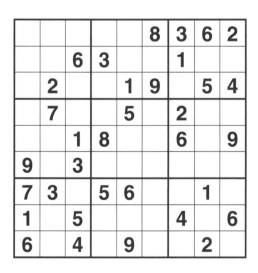

		8	9					
	1	3		6	7			
	9	3		1		6	5	
1		4	6		5	9		7
7	6						2	3
3		9	2		1	4		5
	4	7		6		8	3	
		2	7		4	5		
			5		3			

507 SUDOKU

	2					7		
	9	3				4	2	
5		1		7		9		8
	3	2	5	1	8	6	9	
			7		4			
	7	8	3	6	2	5	1	
6		7		2		3		9
	1	9				2	8	
	8					5		

508 SUDOKU

				8	3	6	2	
		6	3		1			
	2			1	9		5	4
	7			5		2		
		1	8			6		9
9		3						
7	3		5	6			1	
1		5				4		6
6		4		9			2	

509 SUDOKU

		2	9		5	6		
		4	8		2	5		
7	9						2	8
6	7			2			5	1
			1		6			
3	5			4			6	2
2	4						9	5
		6	2		7	8		
		7	5		4	2		

510 SUDOKU

7	2			5		4		3
3		6					8	7
	9					5	6	
			7			1	2	
1				2	4	7	5	
				1				
2		3	6	7			1	4
	1	7	4	9		8		
9	4					6		

511 SUDOKU

			3	6	5			
	3	6		4		1	7	
8	2		9		1		5	3
	7					3		
		2	3	7				
	1						4	
9	5		7		6		1	4
	6	3		8		5	2	
			5	1	3			

512 SUDOKU

		2	1	5		4		
	3			2		5	1	8
	1			8		2	7	
	5	8	9		4			
				1		9		5
	8	7	5		2	1		6
		5	7				2	9
		4			8	7	5	

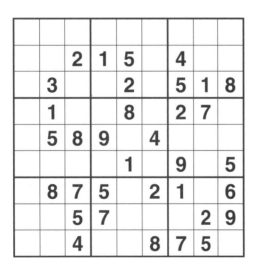

513 SUDOKU

						7		
	9		4				8	
8		7		1	6	2	9	
5				3	2	9	7	6
6					9			
7				5	8	1	2	4
9		1		8	5	4	6	
	6		9				3	
						8		

514 SUDOKU

			6	1	5			
3	9		7		8		4	5
		5		9		6		
6	3						1	7
		8				9		
1	2						5	8
		1		3		8		
2	7		1		4		6	9
			5	6	7			

515 SUDOKU

2		4		9			1	
			1		6			
6		3	4	5		7		
5			9	1				
	4	7	6		8	1	5	
			7	5				9
	5		6	3	9			1
		2		9				
	7			8		6		4

516 SUDOKU

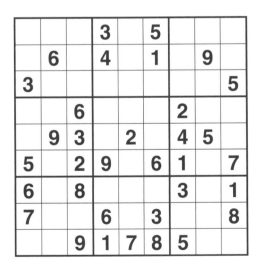

			3		5			
	6		4		1		9	
3								5
		6			2			
	9	3		2		4	5	
5		2	9		6	1		7
6		8				3		1
7			6		3			8
		9	1	7	8	5		

517 SUDOKU

								5
			9	8	6	4		
9				2		4		8
6			1	3		2	4	
	1				5		7	
3		8	4		7	6	5	
1		5	8					
7				6				
2	6	4	5			1	3	

518 SUDOKU

		8	7			9		
			2		1			
3	7		6		9		1	5
		3				6		
9			3	5	4			1
1								9
		6	4		5	1		
4	8						9	6
2	9		1		8		3	7

519 SUDOKU

		9				3		
	4	3	8		6	1	5	
5	2	8				4	6	7
		5	6	4	7	2		
3								8
		2	3	1	8	7		
2	5	6				9	1	3
	8	4	9		2	5	7	
		7				8		

520 SUDOKU

7								4
		8				3		
		5	2		1	8		
		3	8		9	1		
8	1	4				2	5	9
2								8
		9	3	1	7	5		
		2	4	8	5	7		
		1	9		2	4		

521 SUDOKU

		4		3		5		
	5		9	8				6
3			4			2		9
	6	7	1			9		
2			9					
	1	9	5			6		
7			6			8		5
	2		7	1				3
	6		2			9		

522 SUDOKU

		8	4		1	7		
			8	5	7			
	1						9	
5	7						4	8
2	4						1	6
			5		4			
	9						5	
	6	1				3	8	
8	5		6		9		7	1

523 SUDOKU

								7
	9	5	3					
				6		8		4
	4	7	9	2			6	
9	3		1		4		7	8
	8			3	6	1	4	
6		3		1				
					5	9	1	
7								

524 SUDOKU

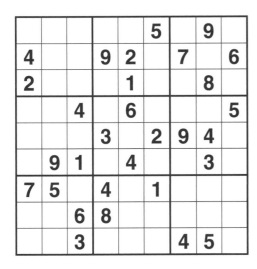

				5		9		
4			9	2		7		6
2				1			8	
		4		6				5
			3		2	9	4	
	9	1		4			3	
7	5			4		1		
		6	8					
		3				4	5	

525 SUDOKU

		1	8					
	5			3		7		
6	3	9					2	
	8	5	7	6				
		2		4		7		
	7	3		1	8			4
9			1		6	3		5
		5		9	4	6		
	4			2				

526 SUDOKU

5		6						
				9		1	5	
			6		7	2		3
1	7					9	2	
		3	9				4	5
2	4					6	3	
			5		4	8		7
				2		3	6	
4		7						

527 SUDOKU

	3			2				
8			4			9		
	9		8	1			7	
	2		3	7				9
		9		2	1	3		
			6		8	4	1	
3	6			4				
2		7			6	8		4
	4	1				2		

528 SUDOKU

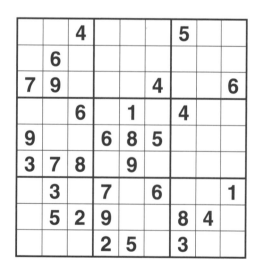

		4			5			
	6							
7	9			4				6
		6		1		4		
9			6	8	5			
3	7	8		9				
	3		7		6			1
	5	2	9			8	4	
			2	5		3		

529 SUDOKU

			8			6		
				2	1			
			3	6	5	2	4	
		5		4	9			
7		9				4		
	3	1	8			6	7	
	7	3	2		8			
1		6		4	3			7
		4				8	1	

530 SUDOKU

3			4		5			9
7		9	1		6	2		5
5	8		3		7		2	4
	6						5	
4	3		6		1		7	8
2		4	8		9	3		7
6			7		4			1

531 SUDOKU

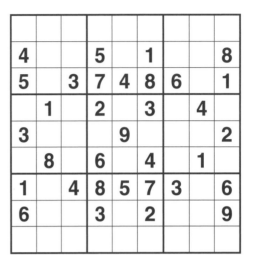

4			5		1			8
5		3	7	4	8	6		1
	1		2		3		4	
3				9				2
	8		6		4		1	
1		4	8	5	7	3		6
6			3		2			9

532 SUDOKU

			7		4			
5		8				1		9
	2	4				7	6	
	5		9		7		3	
4			1		6			7
	8		5		2		1	
	9	5				3	8	
2		7				6		4
			2		9			

533 SUDOKU

	5		8		4		1	
7								2
			2	6	5			
5		7	1		8	4		6
		6				9		
4		8	5		6	2		1
			6	3	7			
2								5
	1		9		2		4	